growth

DISCOVER DISCIPLESHIP
WORKBOOK 3: DISCOVER GROWTH

Jay Morgan

Discover Discipleship Series:
Work Book Three: Discover Growth
© **Jay Morgan 2019**

Editors: Heidi Wallenborn and Wendy Smith

ISBN 979-8-9856015-2-7
Printed in the United States of America

Published by: APC Ministries
www.apcwv.com

table of contents

getting the most from this study

We are glad that you have chosen to pursue this course of study and hope that you are looking forward to beginning. Before you dig in, there are three important things to take into account:

SMALL DAILY INVESTMENT

To get the maximum benefit from this course of study, a 10-15 minute investment to complete a lesson each day is recommended.

Small choices we make each day create the lives we live. Your commitment to spending a few minutes every day to think, journal, study and learn, is a commitment to planting and watering seeds of change.

By doing this, you are creating a harvest of good fruit in your life for yourself and for others to benefit from over time. Even if you do not continue this study, forming the habit of taking time for daily personal growth will benefit you for the rest of your life.

WEEKLY DISCUSSION WITH OTHERS

Each journey that you take in life, whether physical or spiritual, is more enjoyable when you have companions. Someone may see something that you missed or have an idea that is different than your own. Travel is almost always safer in groups.

Likewise, we encourage you to meet regularly with another person or a group of people to discuss thoughts. Spend time with someone who is further down the spiritual road so that you can learn from and lean on them as you progress along your own path. This road is too serious for you to travel upon alone.

MORE THAN A STUDY

This workbook is the third in a series of six. You will find that the six core discoveries as put forth in this series will serve you well beyond this study. These core discoveries are to be used as guides for your spiritual journey, and the workbooks will serve as reference guides throughout your lifetime. This content doesn't end with the course.

Also, keep in mind that each of the six workbooks in this series builds upon each other. It is imperative that you study them in order – and completely – to get the most from this study.

May God bless you as you increase in your knowledge of Him.

Pastor Jay Morgan

For ongoing support and conversations around the topics contained in the *Discover Discipleship Course*, join our online discussion by searching "Discover Discipleship Tribe" on Facebook.

group guidelines

If you are completing this Study in a group setting, the following guidelines will help keep meetings safe, focused and productive:

GROUP LOGISTICS

Appropriate group size. Ideally a group should consist of 4-6 people: a group leader and apprentice leader who have both previously completed the *Discover Discipleship Course,* and 3-4 new participants. If a group is larger, consider discussing key concepts from the lessons together, and then forming smaller break-out groups to discuss the questions.

Meet consistently. During the first meeting the group should agree upon a day/time each week for the meeting. Weekly meetings are ideal. Avoid routinely canceling meetings.

Plan the material. Decide each week how many days/lessons you will want to work on at the next meeting. It is recommended that you cover 3-5 lessons at each weekly group meeting.

Be prepared. Both the leader and participants should fully engage with each week's planned material, and answer all questions *before* the group meeting.

MEETING LOGISTICS

Meeting agenda. Begin each meeting by briefly connecting with everyone. Read the meeting ground rules (on the next page) and pray. Summarize lesson points, one lesson at a time, and allow ample time to discuss the lesson questions. The questions are key to the effectiveness of this study.

Group Prayer. End each group meeting with a time of extended prayer when possible. Worship together a few minutes and then pray for each other's needs. These times of prayer will most likely develop more after *Workbook 3: Discover Growth.*

Meeting length. Weekly meetings should typically last 1 to 1 1/2 hours. Make sure to always start and *end* the meeting on time. People might want to stay longer than originally planned, however, be mindful that members might have other obligations after the scheduled meeting time.

MEETING GROUND RULES

To help keep meetings focused, safe and productive, begin every meeting by reading these ground rules aloud.

1. **I will commit to make group meetings and this study a priority by being prepared and being on time.** The group meeting is not the time to work on answers to questions. I understand the group meeting will be unproductive if I have not read the lessons and answered the questions before the group meeting.

2. **I will maintain confidentiality.** What is said in the group stays in the group unless someone threatens to hurt themselves or others. In that case, appropriate people will be notified to ensure the safety of all parties involved.

3. **I will refrain from gossiping about others during the group meeting.** I will keep my focus on my experiences and not on other people. I will leave others' names anonymous when sharing my negative personal experiences in the group setting.

4. **I will be honest.** The purpose of this study is to give honest answers and work toward the study of God's truth. Everyone is here to discover God's truth together. We cannot discover truth until we ask questions and seek answers.

5. **I will respect the other members of the group.** I will refrain from being on electronic devices, interrupting others and/or having side conversations.

6. **I understand that my role is not to "save" or "fix" anyone else.** Together, our role is to continue to point each other toward Jesus and the truth of His teachings.

Go to the *Church Leader Resources* section of **www.discoverdiscipleship. com** for additional resources to assist with leading a productive group meeting.

introduction to growth

I am the vine; you are the branches. If you remain in me and I in you, you will bear much fruit; apart from me you can do nothing. **– JOHN** 15:5

the growth decision

Congratulations on making it to the third Core Decision of your spiritual journey. We're glad you've chosen to continue this study and hope you're looking forward to discovering more spiritual truths.

REVIEW

In *Workbook 1: Discover Identity*, we learned that we are created in God's image as His children. God desires to have a family to share eternity with. Because of sin, we have all experienced spiritual death. This spiritual death brings physical death and eternal separation from God. Because we have lost our identity as God's children, we seek security, worth and fulfillment from alternative sources—people, things, or even our own self-perception. This search leads us further into sin and away from God.

Motivated by His love for us, God came to us through Jesus and did everything possible to restore us to Himself. When we surrender our will to Jesus' Lordship, the Holy Spirit comes into us and rebirths the child of God in us. Our sins are forgiven, and we are restored to a relationship with God. Remember, as a spiritually reborn child of God, we have new desires and interests.

As a child of God you will desire the following:

- More of God and less of sin. (Galatians 5:17)

- Intimacy with the Father and the nourishment of the Word of God. (Romans 8:15-16, 1 Peter 2:2)

- The community of God's family. (Ephesians 2:19)

- To bear the image of God in the world and do the works you were created to do. (Ephesians 2:8-10, Matthew 28:18-20)

- To honor God with all of your life and resources. (1 Corinthians 6:19-20)

The purpose of the *Discover Discipleship Course* is to help you develop these desires. God placed them in you, but you must cooperate with God and allow these desires to mature and grow in you. Living in your identity as God's child and allowing these desires to develop will help you discover true security, worth and fulfillment.

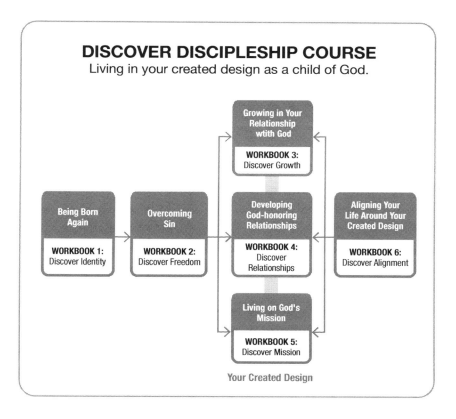

In *Workbook 2: Discover Freedom*, we learned that although we have been spiritually reborn as God's children, we still have spiritual strongholds—old, destructive, sinful desires. These strongholds form over a lifetime of allowing substitute identities, rather than our identity as God's child, to define us.

We must cooperate with the Holy Spirit to experience freedom from these strongholds. By taking *personal responsibility* for change, seeking God's *power* to change, finding *partners* to support our change and developing a *plan* for change, we can experience freedom from spiritual strongholds.

THE GROWTH DECISION

Being spiritually reborn and experiencing freedom from sin is not the end of our spiritual journey, it is just the beginning. In the same way a baby's growth requires the nurture and protection of a parent or caregiver, nurture from an intimate relationship with your Heavenly Father is necessary for your spiritual growth.

You were created for an intimate relationship with God. Jesus described loving God as the greatest commandment.

> One of them, an expert in the law, tested him with this question: "Teacher, which is the greatest commandment in the Law?"
>
> Jesus replied: "'Love the Lord your God with all your heart and with all your soul and with all your mind.' This is the first and greatest commandment." —**Matthew 22:35-38**

This passage indicates a strong passionate love for God—a desire to know Him more. As we've learned, the child of God in you desires intimacy with the Father and nourishment from the Word of God.

In this Workbook you will learn how to grow spiritually and to develop and experience a real relationship with God by making the next Core Decision of your spiritual journey.

The Growth Decision:
I choose to spiritually grow by engaging with God's Presence through prayer and worship and by engaging with His written Word—the Bible.

developing a relationship with God

Although we were created for God, the reality of having a relationship with the Almighty God of the universe can feel impossible. God can seem distant, unseen and unknowable. But remember that God came to you. He *initiated* a relationship with you through Christ.

> For God was in Christ, reconciling the world to himself, no longer counting people's sins against them. And he gave us this wonderful message of reconciliation. —II Corinthians 5:19 NLT

1. How does it make you feel to know that God actively initiated a relationship with you through Christ?

THE HOLY SPIRIT'S ROLE IN THE RELATIONSHIP

God not only initiated a relationship with you through Christ, He continues to initiate a relationship with you through the Holy Spirit.

> And I will ask the Father, and he will give you another advocate to help you and be with you forever — the Spirit of truth. The world cannot accept him, because it neither sees him nor knows him. But you know him, for he lives with you and will be in you. I will not leave you as orphans; I will come to you. —**John 14:16-18**

Reread the previous Scripture passage and notice that Jesus said *He* would actually come to you through the Holy Spirit.

This means that to develop and grow a relationship with God, you must first realize He is not in some distant place. If you have surrendered your life to Christ, He lives with you — He lives inside you — through the Holy Spirit.

The word *advocate* in the previous passage can also be translated *comforter*. This title is from a Greek word that means *to call to one's aid*, which defines what the Holy Spirit does. He comes to our aid.[1]

We can see that God comes to our aid in several ways. He invites us, even implores us, because He desires a relationship with us. He will exhort (urge) us and also comfort us. He assures us that we are God's children. He teaches us how to pray. He guides us into truth.[2]

> But when he, the Spirit of truth, comes, he will guide you into all the truth. He will not speak on his own; he will speak only what he hears, and he will tell you what is yet to come.
> —John 16:13

2. How does it make you feel to know that God continues to initiate a relationship with you through the Holy Spirit?

YOUR PART IN THE RELATIONSHIP

As in all relationships, your relationship with God requires intention and effort from both parties. God has done His part by coming to you and initiating the relationship. If you want the relationship to grow, you must do your part to engage with Him.

> Come near to God and he will come near to you. —James 4:8a

Jesus taught that growing in your relationship with God and fulfilling God's purposes are natural results of staying connected to Him. In other words, if you want to grow in your relationship with God and do what He desires, you must stay close to Him and allow His power and life to flow through you.

> I am the vine; you are the branches. If you remain in me and I in you, you will bear much fruit; apart from me you can do nothing. If you do not remain in me, you are like a branch that is thrown away and withers; such branches are picked up, thrown into the fire and burned. —John 15:5-6

3. What do you think it means to "remain" in Christ?

notes

the Holy Spirit

And I will ask the Father, and he will give you another advocate to help you and be with you forever —the Spirit of truth. — JOHN 14:16-17a NLT

the Holy Spirit's work

Scripture teaches that the Holy Spirit works in our lives in at least three ways:

*   Saving

*   Transforming

*   Empowering

THE SAVING WORK OF THE HOLY SPIRIT

You came to Jesus because of the Holy Spirit's saving work in your life. The Holy Spirit is active in the world, convicting people of sin and drawing them to Jesus.

> And when he comes, he will convict the world of its sin, and of God's righteousness, and of the coming judgment. —**John 16:8 NLT**

> No one can come to me unless the Father who sent me draws them, and I will raise them up at the last day. —**John 6:44**

The Holy Spirit births a new creation — a child of God in you.
When you surrender to Jesus, the Holy Spirit produces spiritual life in you. He takes out your old-nature heart and places a new nature inside you. He lives in you to give you the ability to live in obedience to God.

> Humans can reproduce only human life, but the Holy Spirit gives birth to spiritual life.
> —John 3:6 NLT

And I will give you a new heart, and I will
put a new spirit in you. I will take out your
stony, stubborn heart and give you a tender,
responsive heart. And I will put my Spirit in
you so that you will follow my decrees and be
careful to obey my regulations.
—**Ezekiel 36:26-27 NLT**

If you are spiritually reborn, the Holy Spirit gives you assurance that you are a child of God.

The Spirit you received does not make you
slaves, so that you live in fear again; rather,
the Spirit you received brought about your
adoption to sonship. And by him we cry,
"Abba, Father." The Spirit himself testifies with
our spirit that we are God's children.
—**Romans 8:15-16**

1. **What do you think it means to have assurance that you
    are a child of God?**

2. **Do you have this assurance? If not, pray and ask for
    the assurance of salvation in your heart.**

THE TRANSFORMING WORK OF THE HOLY SPIRIT

The Holy Spirit does not only save you; He applies God's transforming power to your life. Transformation means *change*. This means that the Holy Spirit will not leave you the same. He actively works to produce the desires of God in you. He conforms you into the image of Jesus.

> For God is working in you, giving you the desire and the power to do what pleases him.
> —**Philippians 2:13 NLT**

> For those God foreknew he also predestined to be conformed to the image of his Son, that he might be the firstborn among many brothers and sisters. —**Romans 8:29**

The transforming work of the Holy Spirit is often referred to as the fire of God. This is the power of God that removes sins and impurities from us.

> I [John] baptize you with water for repentance. But after me comes one who is more powerful than I, whose sandals I am not worthy to carry. He will baptize you with the Holy Spirit and fire. —**Matthew 3:11**

The transforming work of the Holy Spirit can restore all parts of our being to a state of wholeness or healing. A simple definition for healing is *to restore things to how they should be.* This includes healing our spirit, body, mind, emotions and relationships.

> He forgives all my sins and heals all my diseases. —**Psalm 103:3 NLT**

Transformation comes through submitting to and cooperating with the Holy Spirit. While Scripture commands us to actively resist the devil, it's a mistake to assume change is based solely upon our efforts. The Holy Spirit is the Power who will transform you. Remember that Scripture teaches that you can cooperate with the Spirit and let Him change you, or you can quench His transforming work in you and grieve Him.

> Do not quench the Spirit.
> —1 Thessalonians 5:19

> And do not grieve the Holy Spirit of God, with whom you were sealed for the day of redemption. —Ephesians 4:30

3. **In which area(s) of your life, do you currently need to experience the transforming power of the Holy Spirit?**

4. **What do you think it means to quench or grieve the Holy Spirit's work in your life?**

THE EMPOWERING WORK OF THE HOLY SPIRIT

The work of God in your life didn't end with your salvation. Salvation is just the beginning. You were saved to complete a mission — to do good works that glorify God.

> For it is by grace you have been saved, through faith — and this is not from yourselves, it is the gift of God — not by works, so that no one can boast. For we are God's handiwork, created in Christ Jesus to do good works, *which God prepared in advance for us to do. (Emphasis added)*
> —**Ephesians 2:8-10**

The Holy Spirit also gives you the power and boldness to share God's Good News.

> But you will receive power when the Holy Spirit comes on you; and you will be my witnesses in Jerusalem, and in all Judea and Samaria, and to the ends of the earth.
> —**Acts 1:8**

The Holy Spirit continues His empowering work in you by placing gifts, or spiritual abilities, in your life. In *Workbook 6: Discover Alignment*, you will learn much more about spiritual gifts. For now, you should understand the following:

- God brings gifts into your life through His Holy Spirit.

- We do not all receive the same gifts, but we all receive the same Spirit.

- God decides which gifts to give based on the job He has for you.

- You should be open to receive any gift God desires to give you.

All these [spiritual gifts] are the work of one
and the same Spirit, and he distributes them to
each one, just as he determines.
—1 Corinthians 12:11

**Through the Holy Spirit, the very power that raised Jesus
from the dead is in you.**

I also pray that you will understand the
incredible greatness of God's power for us who
believe him. This is the same mighty power that
raised Christ from the dead and seated him in
the place of honor at God's right hand in the
heavenly realms. —**Ephesians 1:19-20 NLT**

5. **How does it make you feel to know that the power that
raised Christ from the dead lives in you?**

receiving the Holy Spirit

The Jews in Jesus' time believed that the Messiah —the one sent from God to save them —would baptize people.[3]

> Now the Pharisees who had been sent questioned him, "Why then do you baptize if you are not the Messiah, nor Elijah, nor the Prophet?" —**John 1:24-25**

To baptize literally means to *immerse*. It was a custom for people to be immersed in water to signify change. It was symbolic of washing away an old belief.

John, the one who announced Jesus' identity to the world, stated that Jesus — the true Messiah—would not baptize people with water. He would baptize them with the Holy Spirit and fire. In other words, the Holy Spirit of God, not water, is the substance in which Jesus immerses His people.

> I baptize you with water for repentance. But after me comes one who is more powerful than I, whose sandals I am not worthy to carry. He will baptize you with the Holy Spirit and fire.
> —**Matthew 3:11**

Throughout His ministry recorded in Scripture, we can see that Jesus didn't baptize people with water. His disciples did, and He commanded us to; but He did not.

> ...it was not Jesus who baptized, but his disciples. —**John 4:2**

After Jesus returned to heaven, Peter taught that Jesus is even now pouring out God's Holy Spirit on all humanity. Christ is baptizing — immersing — us in God's Spirit.

> In the last days, God says, I will pour out my Spirit on all people…
>
> God has raised this Jesus to life, and we are all witnesses of it. Exalted to the right hand of God, he has received from the Father the promised Holy Spirit and has poured out what you now see and hear. —**Acts 2:17, 32-33**

Peter knew this was the Holy Spirit being poured out by Jesus, because Jesus had promised they would be baptized with the Holy Spirit.

> On one occasion, while he was eating with them, he gave them this command: "Do not leave Jerusalem, but wait for the gift my Father promised, which you have heard me speak about. For John baptized with water, but in a few days you will be baptized with the Holy Spirit." —**Acts 1:4-5**

Scripture teaches that when this baptism occurred, the disciples were also filled with the Holy Spirit.

> When the day of Pentecost came, they were all together in one place. Suddenly a sound like the blowing of a violent wind came from heaven and filled the whole house where they were sitting. They saw what seemed to be tongues of fire that separated and came to rest on each of them. All of them were filled with the Holy Spirit and began to speak in other tongues as the Spirit enabled them. —**Acts 2:1-4**

THE HOLY SPIRIT UPON YOU AND IN YOU

The Holy Spirit upon you. In the Book of Acts there are several accounts of when the Holy Spirit "fell on," "came upon," or was "poured out on" people. All these accounts imply that the Holy Spirit was around or upon people. They were immersed — baptized — in the Holy Spirit.[4]

If you're concerned that the early church's experience doesn't describe anything that has happened to you, don't misunderstand. People are often baptized with the Holy Spirit but don't recognize it. If you've ever felt what you believed was God's Spirit coming upon you, surrounding you, "hugging" or overwhelming you; if you have experienced a deep sense of peace come upon you through prayer; it's likely you experienced "baptism" in God's Spirit.

1. Describe a time you felt God around you or upon you.

The Holy Spirit in you. Scripture states that you have a receptive role to play when the Holy Spirit comes upon you. As noted before, Luke, in the Book of Acts, detailed several accounts of the Holy Spirit being around or upon people, but he also detailed accounts of the Holy Spirit being in people after He was upon them.[5]

Twice in Acts, Luke describes people "receiving" the Holy Spirit, and five times he describes people being "filled" after the Holy Spirit came upon them. The Holy Spirit was not just *on* them. He was *in* them.

Think of it this way: If you stand under a waterfall, the water is on you and all around you. You are in essence "immersed" in the water. If you open your mouth the water "fills" you. You receive the water into yourself.

Notice how Scripture describes these encounters with the Holy Spirit. The Spirit would come upon people and then the person allowed Him to fill them. In this Scriptural context, to be filled also means to be controlled. It implies a complete surrender to the Spirit's work in your life.

This first happened when you initially surrendered to Jesus' Lordship. God's Spirit was active and drew your heart to the message. You had to respond, surrender and receive it. When you did, the Holy Spirit entered into you and you were born again as a child of God.

The Holy Spirit was not just working around you, you had to allow Him to enter you and work in you. The following verse states that God actually removes your old heart, gives you a new one, and then resides in you.

> And I will give you a new heart, and I will
> put a new spirit in you. I will take out your
> stony, stubborn heart and give you a tender,
> responsive heart. And I will put my Spirit in
> you so that you will follow my decrees and be
> careful to obey my regulations.
> —Ezekiel 36:26-27 NLT

On *Day 2: Developing a Relationship with God* we learned that God's Holy Spirit is Christ Himself (John 14:16-18). Christ is pouring Himself out on the entire world. By pouring Himself out on all humanity, He makes Himself available to everyone. But we must open up our hearts, minds and spirits to receive Him and allow Him to accomplish His work in our lives.

2. **Describe the difference between the Holy Spirit being around or upon you, and the Holy Spirit being in you.**

the ongoing work of the Holy Spirit

Peter taught that if people repented and were baptized, they would receive the gift of the Holy Spirit.

> Peter replied, "Repent and be baptized every one of you, in the name of Jesus Christ for the forgiveness of your sins. And you will receive the gift of the Holy Spirit… Those who accepted his message were baptized, and about three thousand were added to their number that day.
> —**Acts 2:38, 41**

This Scripture implies that people received the Holy Spirit after they repented and were baptized.

Later in the book of Acts, the believers had multiple, tangible encounters with the Holy Spirit. These encounters with the Holy Spirit were recurring experiences in the lives of surrendered believers.

At least three different times Peter was in a group that was "filled" again (Acts 2:3-4; Acts 4:8; Acts 4:31). This means that the experience of receiving the Holy Spirit's baptism and infilling is not limited to only one occurrence or to our initial conversion experience. Notice the following verse:

> Don't be drunk with wine, because that will ruin your life. Instead, be filled with the Holy Spirit. —**Ephesians 5:18 NLT**

"Be filled with the Holy Spirit" in this verse can be translated, *keep on being filled with the Holy Spirit*.[6] Any translation of the verse suggests that being filled with the Spirit is an ongoing process. You should do this as a daily process of submitting to the control and influence of the Holy Spirit.

This does not mean that you should be in constant fear of "losing" God's Spirit. It means you should allow the Holy Spirit to sustain you continually, and then when necessary, He will empower you to do what you cannot accomplish through your power.

Think of it this way: We all have adrenal glands in our bodies. Their job is to maintain homeostasis — a big word for balance — which gives us the energy we need to function. Without them, we would be lifeless. When necessary, they pump a large amount of adrenaline into our bodies and give us power to do more than we could previously do. Have you heard of a mother lifting a car off her child? It was the result of adrenaline empowering her to do what needed to be done, even though it seemed impossible.

In the same way, the Holy Spirit is always at work in us, giving us spiritual life and accomplishing His work in us. However, when needed, He can instantly empower us, through a tangible encounter, for a specific work or task.[7]

These divine encounters can happen while others pray with you or while you are in personal prayer. They can happen in public or in private. Their distinguishing mark is a definitive change in your life *after* the encounter.

1. **Why should you pray to be consistently refilled with the Holy Spirit?**

DIVINE PROCESS VERSUS DIVINE ENCOUNTERS

Some people insist that God only accomplishes His work instantly, while others argue that He only works gradually. Scripture proposes both.

Divine process refers to the way God gradually accomplishes His work in your life. Divine encounter refers to the way God instantly accomplishes His work in your life.

On *Day 3: The Holy Spirit's Work* we learned about three works of the Holy Spirit in a believer's life. Now let's explore how the Holy Spirit can accomplish these three works in our lives through divine *process* and divine *encounters*.

The Saving Work. This work was accomplished when you believed and surrendered your life to Jesus; you are saved and the Holy Spirit lives in you (Acts 2:38). The saving work happens instantly but is often the result of a process of the Holy Spirit leading you toward Christ.

The Transforming Work. At the moment of your salvation, or after another encounter with the Holy Spirit, you may have experienced immediate freedom from a particular sin, or experienced healing in your body.

Other times freedom or healing comes through a process of leaning on Him while you daily surrender to His power. Pray for instantaneous healing and freedom, but if it does not immediately come, allow Him to change you through the process of surrendering to His will.

The Empowering Work. Sometimes the Holy Spirit will place power and abilities in your life through an instant divine encounter. The writer of the book of Acts gives several examples of this. Sometimes the believers spoke in unknown tongues (Acts 2:3-4), and at times prophesied (Acts 19:6). Other times they spoke the Word boldly (Acts 4:31). Some received power to face death or difficult situations with confidence. (Acts 7:54-60). You, too, might have experienced a time when the Holy Spirit *instantly* empowered you to do what you could not typically do.

At other times, you're not sure when certain gifts or confidence came into your life. They become apparent after time spent in God's Presence. Notice that the empowering work accomplished in the disciples on the day of Pentecost came after several days of waiting in prayer. This implies that God was performing His empowering work through the process of waiting in prayer, as well as through an instant divine encounter on the day of Pentecost (Acts 1 and 2).

NOTE: On *Day 9: Experiencing God's Presence* we will learn more about physical and emotional reactions to the Presence of the Holy Spirit. While it's possible to speculate and debate about the authenticity of people's encounters with the Holy Spirit, the real test is the results: Are there Christ-like changes in the person's life?

2. **Have you experienced a divine encounter that instantly produced forgiveness, healing, freedom, spiritual gifts or empowerment in your life? If yes, describe the occurrence.**

3. **Have you noticed that forgiveness, healing, freedom, spiritual gifts or empowerment have come to you over a period of time? If yes, describe one of these.**

notes

worship and prayer

Come close to God, and God will come close to you…
—JAMES 4:8a

understanding worship

The Holy Spirit is the Spirit of God living in you. He desires to have a relationship with you and to interact with you. He desires to give love to you, and to receive love from you. The word *worship* is often used to describe this process of expressing love to and receiving love from God.

Experiencing the Presence of God through prayer and worship is a vital part of your relationship with Him. As in all other relationships, love grows by spending time together. Notice how the psalmist described his desire to spend time worshipping God:

> One thing I ask from the Lord, this only do I seek: that I may dwell in the house of the Lord all the days of my life, to gaze on the beauty of the Lord and to seek him in his temple.
> —**Psalm 27:4**

There are several things we can learn about worship from this passage:

Worship is being in the Presence of God. In order to be in God's Presence, you do not need to go to a particular building, such as the Tabernacle or Temple in Old Testament worship. God does not live in buildings.

> The God who made the world and everything in it is the Lord of heaven and earth and does not live in temples built by human hands.
> —**Acts 17:24**

Although we gather in buildings to worship God with others, His Presence is not limited to any structure. You can experience Him in public or in private — in a building or outside. The Presence of God is a spiritual place we enter.

Although we may need to make an intentional effort to be *aware* that we are in God's Presence, we do not need to strive or work to get there. Jesus made it possible for us to enter directly into God's Presence. God and man are no longer separated.

> For we do not have a high priest who is unable to empathize with our weaknesses, but we have one who has been tempted in every way, just as we are — yet he did not sin. Let us then approach God's throne of grace with confidence, so that we may receive mercy and find grace to help us in our time of need.
> —Hebrews 4:15-16

1. What does it mean to say that the Presence of God is a spiritual place that we enter?

2. What does it mean to make an intentional effort to be aware that we are in God's Presence?

3. **What are some things that you can do during public worship to become more aware of God's Presence and worth? During private worship?**

Worship is a response to God's worth and beauty. Although it is often misdirected, the desire to worship and praise is part of our nature. Have you noticed how effortless it is to tell others about a good restaurant or movie, encouraging them to experience it as well? C.S. Lewis explored this natural tendency to praise in his book *Reflections on the Psalms*:

> *The most obvious fact about praise—whether of God or anything—strangely escaped me. I had never noticed that all enjoyment spontaneously overflows into praise unless…shyness or the fear of boring others is deliberately brought in to check it.*
>
> *I had not noticed either that just as men spontaneously praise whatever they value, so they spontaneously urge us to join them in praising it.*
>
> *I think we delight to praise what we enjoy because the praise not merely expresses but completes the enjoyment; it is its appointed consummation. It is not out of compliment that lovers keep on telling one another how beautiful they are; the delight is incomplete until it is expressed.*
>
> *The Scotch catechism says that man's chief end is "to glorify God and enjoy Him forever." But we shall then know that these are the same thing. Fully to enjoy is to glorify. In commanding us to glorify Him, God is inviting us to enjoy Him.*[8]

This means that when we learn to truly enjoy our relationship with God, it naturally results with expressed praise and love for God.

4. Why does enjoyment overflow into praise?

5. If we express praise for earthly things, how much more should we be compelled to express our love for God?

6. What does it say about your relationship with God if it does not naturally overflow into expressions of love and praise?

Worship is a decision. It can be easy to make the mistake of believing that worship is only a response to feeling or sensing God's Presence—which means you only express worship if a certain feeling comes over you. Although one can definitely experience the Presence of God, (more about this on *Day 9: Experiencing God's Presence*) worship is also about *initiating* an encounter with Him.

In other words, you should express worship whether or not you feel like it. Worship can be simply defined as *assigning worth.* When we worship God, we acknowledge His worth, His value. We worship because we understand that God is God and He is worthy of our worship. We do not worship based on our feelings in the moment.

Worship involves a decision to look past our feelings and circumstances to see the glory and beauty of God. When we do this, we are gripped by His infinite beauty and will want to worship and praise! The problem is never a lack of God's glory or worth; the problem lies in our perception of God's glory and worth.

Focusing and seeing His worth and glory is not always easy. Our human nature often clouds our ability to see and weakens our desire to pursue God. This is why Scripture encourages us to continually bring God a sacrifice of praise.

> Through Jesus, therefore, let us continually offer to God a sacrifice of praise — the fruit of lips that openly profess his name.
> —**Hebrews 13:15**

Continually means we must worship in all circumstances. *A sacrifice of praise* suggests we must intentionally open our mouths and speak of the goodness of God, even if—particularly if—we do not feel like it.

This does not mean we can never acknowledge that we have a problem. This means we must choose to openly express and declare Who God is, despite our problems. Worship is a decision to focus on the goodness of God, rather than the pain of our problem.

What enables us to do this? *Jesus*. When we truly encounter Him and choose to focus on Him for Who He truly is, the goodness of God goes without question in our minds. Worship floods out of us.

7.   What does it mean to initiate an encounter with God?

8.   Why should we initiate and express worship whether or not we feel like it?

worship — expressing love to God

Scripture teaches that our entire lives should be lived as an offering of worship to God (Romans 12:1), but it also instructs us to intentionally and actively express our love *to* God. In the same way that human love is expressed through a touch or hug or by saying "I love you," God desires for us to express our love to Him. For the purpose of this discussion we will refer to these active expressions of love as worship.

1. **What is the difference between feeling love and expressing love?**

WORSHIP THAT PLEASES GOD

Scripture teaches several ways to worship and express love to God. We typically express worship to God in ways that are "comfortable" to us or are reflective of our personality. But should these things alone dictate our worship expressions?

In our human relationships, we should seek to express our love to people in ways that are meaningful to the recipient of our love. Some people prefer time alone, others enjoy affectionate touch, while others desire to hear affectionate words spoken to them. When you love the person, you will seek to communicate love in ways that are meaningful to them.[9]

In the same way, you should seek to express love to God in ways that are meaningful to Him. Scripture is full of directions about how God desires us to worship Him. Rather than asking, "*Does this make me feel comfortable?*" we should ask, "*How does God want me to worship Him?*"

If you love Him, you should *desire* to express worship to God in every way that He desires, as directed in Scripture. Your desire in worship should be to please His heart. You shouldn't have to be forced to express love to God.

2. **Should God's desires or your comfort determine your expression of worship? Explain:**

MUSICAL EXPRESSIONS OF WORSHIP

Singing and playing instruments. Singing and playing instruments are powerful ways to express feelings and emotions during personal and public worship. Songs of praise and thanksgiving are sung to declare God's goodness and character. Worship songs are actually sung *to* God, rather than *about* Him. In essence, they are prayers set to music, similar to Old Testament Psalms.

You don't have to sing well to sing to God. If you're leading the singing of public worship, it's helpful to be able to sing well. But Scripture directs all of us to sing to God, not just those who sing well.

> Praise him with the sounding of the trumpet, praise him with the harp and lyre, praise him with timbrel and dancing, praise him with the strings and pipe, praise him with the clash of cymbals, praise him with resounding cymbals.
> —Psalm 150:3-5

> ...speaking to one another with psalms, hymns, and songs from the Spirit. Sing and make music from your heart to the Lord.
> —Ephesians 5:19

Playing recorded worship music during your personal times of devotion can help create a reverent atmosphere and keep your mind focused.

VERBAL EXPRESSIONS OF WORSHIP

Prayer. Prayer is talking to God. Prayer doesn't have to be complicated. It's all right to talk to God using simple language and common words.

> And when you pray, do not keep on babbling like pagans, for they think they will be heard because of their many words.
> —Matthew 6:7

This doesn't mean that prayers can't be long, it simply means that wordiness does not determine the importance of a prayer. We will learn more about prayer on *Day 8: H.E.A.R.T. Guided Prayer.*

Telling people about God and what He has done. C.S. Lewis reminded us that praise is an automatic response to something we love. We praise it and then encourage others to praise it as well. *Isn't that awesome? It's a beautiful day today, isn't it?*[10] When we speak of God's goodness and greatness to others, we are in fact worshipping and praising Him.

> Come, let us tell of the Lord's greatness; let us exalt his name together. —Psalm 34:3 NLT

Repeating worshipful words or phrases. This is speaking simple words or phrases to express love and gratitude to God, such as *I love you, Jesus; Praise God; Hallelujah* (which means praise God), or simply, *Jesus.*

Repeating a phrase doesn't cause God to hear you more, but it can help you focus when you're distracted.

Repeating words or phrases can also help you communicate your love to God when you're not sure what to say. Scripture tells us that repeated phrases of worship are used even in Heaven.

> Day after day and night after night they keep
> on saying, "Holy, holy, holy is the Lord God,
> the Almighty —the one who always was, who
> is, and who is still to come."
> —**Revelation 4:8b NLT**

Shout out joyful praise. Exclamations of praise are a common expression of strong feeling in most cultures of the world. Think of shouting out in joy when your team scores a point. Many faith traditions emphasize quiet, inward worship. While there is great benefit to quiet and reflective worship, shouts of joy and praise are also encouraged in Scripture as a response to God's greatness and mighty acts of power.

> Sing to him a new song; play skillfully, and
> shout for joy. —**Psalm 33:3**

PHYSICAL EXPRESSIONS OF WORSHIP

Actively involving your body in a physical act of worship can help bring your heart and attitude into alignment. Lifting your hands and kneeling or lying down before the Lord can humble your heart. Clapping and dancing can also express deep feelings. Notice the following Scriptural examples and commands to express worship with your body:

Lift your hands to the Lord.

> Let us lift up our hearts and our hands to God
> in heaven... —**Lamentations 3:41**

> Therefore I want the men everywhere to
> pray, lifting up holy hands without anger or
> disputing. —**1 Timothy 2:8**

Kneel down before the Lord.

> Come, let us bow down in worship, let us kneel before the Lord our Maker. —**Psalm 95:6**

Lie down before the Lord.

> All the angels were standing around the throne and around the elders and the four living creatures. They fell down on their faces before the throne and worshiped God.
> —**Revelation 7:11**

> Ezra praised the Lord, the great God; and all the people lifted their hands and responded, "Amen! Amen!" Then they bowed down and worshiped the Lord with their faces to the ground. —**Nehemiah 8:6**

Clap your hands to celebrate the Lord.

> Clap your hands, all you nations; shout to God with cries of joy. —**Psalm 47:1b**

Dance before the Lord.

> Let them praise his name with dancing and make music to him with timbrel and harp.
> —**Psalm 149:3**

3. Which of the worship expressions described are new to you? Which are familiar?

4. Why should you be willing to stretch beyond your comfort zone and express worship in new ways?

PUBLIC WORSHIP CONSIDERATIONS

Although we can worship God wherever we are, we are commanded in Scripture to assemble with other Christians.

> And let us not neglect our meeting together, as some people do, but encourage one another, especially now that the day of his return is drawing near. —**Hebrews 10:25**

Because the primary purpose of public gatherings is for the benefit of the group, not just the individual, Scripture teaches that public worship should be done in a fitting and orderly way (1 Corinthians 14:40). This means with respect and consideration for others.

To be clear, orderly worship does *not* mean only reserved and timid displays of worship are appropriate in public. After all, most worship described in Scripture was in groups of people, and most of those worship celebrations were expressive and bold.

Orderly worship *does* mean that when you engage in public worship you should be sensitive to what God is doing with the entire group, not just in you. One way to do this is to take cues from worship service leaders. If they` encourage Scriptural expressions of worship, it is not inappropriate to express your worship to God in those ways.

Obviously, if you are doing your own thing with no regard for people around you, you could become disorderly and disruptive. However, if active displays of worship are being encouraged and expressed, it can also be disorderly to hold back and refuse to participate.

Do not inhibit your wholehearted expression of worship during appropriate times. Do not allow fear of others' opinion stop you from expressing your worship to God.

5. Review the expressions of worship. Are some expressions more comfortable for you to express in private rather than in public? Which ones—and why? Should it matter?

H.E.A.R.T.
guided prayer

Prayer is perhaps the most common expression of worship to God. Many people are intimidated by prayer, but prayer doesn't have to be complicated. It's alright to talk to God using simple language and common words. Think of prayer as a conversation with God.

TYPES OF PRAYER

Often our prayers could be summarized as *Please* and *Thank You* prayers—only praying when we want God to do something and then occasionally adding a thank you. Scripture lists many different types of prayer. Following are a few:

- **Praise:** (Psalms 145) Declaring the goodness and character of God. *Lord you are great and mighty. You are holy. Who is like our God? You are my Redeemer. You are my Savior. You are my Healer.*

- **Thanksgiving:** (Psalm 138) Thanking God for what He has done for you or others: *Lord thank you for my health. Thank you for forgiving me. Thank you for my family.*

- **Worship:** (Psalm 18:1) Expressing intimate love to God. *Jesus, I Love you. I worship You. Oh Lord, You're beautiful, Your face is all I seek.*[11]

- **Confession:** (Psalms 51) Admitting sin. *God, I am sorry for my sin. Please forgive me for….*

- **Petition/Intercession:** (Psalm 143) Asking for God's intervention. *God please send revival to our land. Please bring healing to… Please help me with…*

As you develop confidence with prayer, you will find it helpful to look up the Scripture passages listed as well as others and read them out loud as your prayer. Most references provided are from the *Book of Psalms* which is a Prayer and Songbook used by the Jewish faith to guide their prayers.

1. **Pause right now and pick a type of prayer listed above. Find the Scriptural example and read it aloud as a prayer to God, then pray your own expression of this type of prayer.**

2. **How did praying the verses impact your prayer? Explain:**

THE LORD'S PRAYER—H.E.A.R.T. PRAYER

In Matthew 6:9-13, Jesus taught His disciples to pray in a certain manner. This is typically called the Lord's Prayer. He did not say to always repeat these particular words when you pray; He said to pray in this *manner* —pray this way. In this prayer He is teaching us the principles of prayer.

> Our Father in heaven, hallowed be your name,
> your kingdom come, your will be done,
> on earth as it is in heaven.
> Give us today our daily bread.
> And forgive us our debts,
> as we also have forgiven our debtors.
> And lead us not into temptation,
> but deliver us from the evil one
> —**Matthew 6:9-13**

A simple way to remember the principles of this prayer is through the *H.E.A.R.T. Model of Prayer*. Take a few minutes *every day* to do this. As you take time to work through the Lord's Prayer, you will find that the time you spend talking with God quickly grows.

Humble yourself before God.

> *Our Father in heaven, hallowed be your name.*

Humble yourself before God and acknowledge His supremacy over all things. It might help to envision God while you lift your hands and kneel or lie down as physical acts of surrender before Him. Remember to add the different expressions of worship you learned on the *Day 7: Worship – Expressing Love to God.*

Thank God and worship Him for who He is and what He has already done in your life. This is the time to participate in worshipful prayer by expressing love and praise to God. This can be as simple as repeating a phrase of love or praise several times to help you focus your mind on His Presence.

Embrace His Will and Kingdom

> *Your kingdom come, your will be done, on earth as it is in heaven.*

Ask for God's desires. In other words, ask God that His will and Kingdom be present in your life and world today.

Ask the Holy Spirit to point out any area of your life that is not submitted to His Lordship (Kingdom). For example, you might resist what you read in the Bible that day; choose to surrender to the Kingdom.

Ask the Holy Spirit to use you to bring His desires into your life and world. Listen carefully during this time. He may direct you to encourage or pray for certain people. He may tell you ways you can help people whom you are praying for. Be alert and open to whatever He asks from you.

Ask for today's provision

Give us today our daily bread.

Identify your worries and one at a time release them into His care. Remember that asking for God's provision does not guarantee things will work out the way you want. You are learning to trust His provision—not your own.

Focus on today's worries and problems. Anxiety often overwhelms us because we stress about potential problems. While it is wise to reasonably prepare for the future, Jesus taught us not to worry about tomorrow. (See Matthew 6:34) Pray for today's provision.

Ask the Holy Spirit to reveal which actions, if any, you should take in each of your areas of worry. Trust His Provision for the things you can do nothing about. Remember to work through your worries one at a time. Do not move forward until you sense release or calmness in that particular area.

Receive and give forgiveness

And forgive us our debts, as we have forgiven our debtors.

Think back through the previous day. Confess any wrong you have done. To confess wrong means you *agree* or *admit* you are wrong. You admit that you are indebted to God and others. It is our nature to hide sin or cover it up. Confession brings sin into the light. You are promised forgiveness if you confess your sin. (See 1 John 1:9)

Prayerfully extend forgiveness to people who have wronged you. Do not push forward through prayer until you get a sense of peace about each person or problem that troubles you. Consider the steps you should take to reconcile with that person. (See Matthew 18:15-17)

Turn away from temptation

And lead us not into temptation, but deliver us from the evil one.

Praying for forgiveness for sin is important. Turning away from temptation that leads to sin is equally important. Think through your day and identify potentially tempting situations. Consider how you can direct your day away from those situations.

If you cannot redirect your day away from the situation, think through a plan to limit the temptation. Specifically, whom will you contact for accountability in this tempting situation? Contact them now. Ask for the Holy Spirit to lead and guide you. (We learned ways to turn away from temptation in *Workbook 2: Discover Freedom.*)

The H.E.A.R.T. pattern of prayer, based upon the Lord's Prayer, is a combination of the different types of prayer listed in the first part of today's lesson. Identify the different types of prayer as you work through it.

3. **Go back through the H.E.A.R.T. prayer and fully engage in it, step by step. Consider writing yours out here or in a separate journal or notebook.**

experiencing God's presence

In previous lessons, we learned that a relationship with God is not one-sided. While you interact with Him, God desires to interact with you.

1. **Is this a new understanding about God's involvement in your life?**

Remember, the Holy Spirit is actually God with you and in you. He desires a relationship with you. It is important to allow time with Him without rushing or doing all the talking.

Sit quietly in His Presence. There is a time to speak prayer to God. There is also a time to quiet your voice and mind and listen to God.

> He says, "Be still, and know that I am God;
> I will be exalted among the nations, I will be
> exalted in the earth." ——**Psalm 46:10**

> Be still before the Lord and wait patiently for
> him. ——**Psalm 37:7a**

Enjoy the peace of God. You may have an overwhelming feeling of peace. If so, slow down and enjoy it.

> And the peace of God, which transcends all
> understanding, will guard your hearts and your
> minds in Christ Jesus. —**Philippians 4:7**

Focus your mind on Jesus. You may find it helpful to think about Jesus while you pray. Think about the cross of Calvary. Allow Jesus to speak to you. Allow Him to comfort you and take away all of your worries and burdens.

> Come to me, all you who are weary and
> burdened, and I will give you rest.
> —**Matthew 11:28**

> Think about the things of heaven, not the things
> of earth. —**Colossians 3:2 NLT**

Listen for the Voice of God. There may be a phrase or a thought or verse going over and over in your mind. Think on it. It could be the Holy Spirit speaking Jesus' truth to you.

> Cause me to understand the way of your
> precepts, that I may meditate on your
> wonderful deeds. —**Psalm 119:27**

> But when he, the Spirit of truth, comes, he will
> guide you into all the truth. He will not speak
> on his own; he will speak only what he hears,
> and he will tell you what is yet to come.
> —**John 16:13**

Allow the Holy Spirit to pray for you. You may sense a deep concern while you pray. You may or may not know what it is about. During these times the Holy Spirit may be praying or interceding for you.

> In the same way, the Spirit helps us in our
> weakness. We do not know what we ought to
> pray for, but the Spirit himself intercedes for us
> through wordless groans. —**Romans 8:26**

2. Have you ever experienced God's Presence in one of the ways described? If yes, describe your experience.

REACTIONS TO THE HOLY SPIRIT'S PRESENCE

The Holy Spirit is not just an idea or a thought or an "it." He is real. When you spend time with Him in worship, He responds to you. Although you may not see Him with your physical eyes, you can sense His Presence. When you do, it's not unusual for your body or emotions to react to Him. These reactions are not the Holy Spirit. These are your body's response to interacting with the Holy Spirit and what He brings. After all, He is the God of the Universe. That's a pretty powerful force!

Emotional reactions are normal. You may feel strong emotions while in the Presence of God. Jesus taught us to worship God with our entire being. This includes our emotions.

> Jesus replied: "Love the Lord your God with all your heart and with all your soul and with all your mind." —**Matthew 22:37**

It is not uncommon for people to laugh or cry when they feel overwhelming peace or joy in God's Presence; feeling emotions is a normal reaction to God's Presence.

> A woman in that town who lived a sinful life learned that Jesus was eating at the Pharisee's house, so she came there with an alabaster jar of perfume. As she stood behind him at his feet weeping, she began to wet his feet with her tears. Then she wiped them with her hair, kissed them and poured perfume on them. —Luke 7:37-38

Physical reactions are normal. It is not uncommon for people to physically sense the Presence of God. Scripture gives several examples of physical reactions to God's Presence being so strong that people were actually unable to stand.

> When I saw him, I fell at his feet as though dead. Then he placed his right hand on me and said: "Do not be afraid. I am the First and the Last." —**Revelation 1:17**

3. **Have you ever reacted emotionally or physically to God's Presence? If yes, describe one of these experiences.**

FOUR CAUTIONS WITH SPIRITUAL EXPERIENCES

Seek a relationship with God, not a particular emotion. You should desire God, not a feeling that may come with being in His Presence. A real relationship is built on more than an emotional experience.

You may experience God's Presence differently than others. We are directed to express worship in similar ways (kneeling, singing, lifting hands, etc.), but our reaction to God's Spirit might be different from others'. It's okay if you don't experience God's Presence the same way others do.

An overemphasis on having a particular experience can lead people to fake their experiences to appear spiritual. Focus on being with God; enjoy Him in any way He chooses to interact with you.

Feeling a particular emotion does not mean God is causing it. Many things can make you feel emotional. Almost any response to God's Spirit can be seen and copied or worked up through other means. This does not mean that God will never produce an emotional or physical reaction. It simply means we should, as Scripture directs, "test" the spirits and see if they are from God (1 John 4:1).

Again, the most important thing is to focus on God and enjoy whatever He brings you.

4. What are your thoughts concerning these four cautions about spiritual experiences?

5. Conclude your time today by sitting quietly in God's Presence. Review and think about the verses and ideas from the "Experiencing God's Presence" section from today.

    Be aware of what you are experiencing.

    Write down some ways in which you believe the Holy Spirit engaged with you during today's time of prayer and listening.

Be prepared to spend time at your next Study Group meeting expressing worship to God and responding to His Presence.

fasting and prayer

Due to general misunderstanding and past church abuses of the practice, fasting is often missing from the life of contemporary Christians. However, prayer combined with fasting has been practiced by the children of God in the Old and New Testaments, and throughout Christian history. The Bible teaches that prayer and fasting are to be part of the life of a believer.

> So we fasted and petitioned our God about this, and he answered our prayer. —Ezra 8:23

NOTE: This lesson is not intended to be medical advice. These are general observations concerning Biblical fasting. Please contact your doctor with any medical questions concerning fasting.

THE PURPOSE OF FASTING

Definition of fasting. Biblical fasting is the act of going without food (or certain foods or activities) for a certain amount of time in order to humble yourself and heighten awareness of your need for God.

Prayer combined with fasting is a discipline that seeks to recapture your hunger for God. It indicates that you are willing to set aside anything to be in His Presence and to hear His Voice.

Richard Foster explains in his book, *Celebration of Discipline*, that fasting and other spiritual disciplines do not in themselves produce change in us, but they place us where change can occur.[12] Fasting and prayer help us place ourselves before God so that He can transform us.

TYPES OF FASTS

Total-Food Fast: In this fast, you do not eat any food and only consume liquids (typically only water or juice) for a specified number of days. Total-food fasts are usually for one to three days. When people engage in an extended, total-food fast (three or more days), they often eat one light, healthy meal each day for the designated fast days.

Partial-food Fast: During this fast, certain foods are given up for a specified number of days. People who desire to fast but cannot do a total-food fast for medical and health reasons will often engage in a partial-food fast.

NOTE: People will also do a combination of a total-food and a partial-food fast for an extended period. For example, a person will fast sweets (partial-food fast) for 21 days but will fast all food (total-food fast) every Tuesday during the 21 days.

The Daniel Fast: The Daniel Fast is a particular type of Biblical partial-food fast. This fast is patterned after two periods of fasting that Daniel engaged in (found in Daniel 1 and Daniel 10). During this type of fast, you primarily eat foods that grow from a seed. This includes fruit, vegetables, grains, seeds, nuts, rice… etc. You also drink water and juice during this fast.[13]

Activities Fast: During this fast people will sacrifice and not engage in television, social media, entertainment, hobbies or other activities they enjoy. This can be done in combination with other types of fasts.

HOW JESUS VIEWED FASTING

Jesus fasted.

> Jesus, full of the Holy Spirit, left the Jordan and was led by the Spirit into the wilderness, where for forty days he was tempted by the devil. He ate nothing during those days, and at the end of them he was hungry. —Luke 4:1-2

Jesus expected His followers to fast. Notice in the following verse, Jesus did not say, "If you fast." He said, "When you fast."

> When you fast, do not look somber as the hypocrites do... —**Matthew 6:16a**

Jesus taught that you should not bring attention to your fast. With that understood, it is Biblically appropriate for a group fast to be called; during those times others will know you are fasting. The point is that you should not go around seeking attention because you are going without food.

> When you fast, do not look somber as the hypocrites do, for they disfigure their faces to show others they are fasting. Truly I tell you, they have received their reward in full. But when you fast, put oil on your head and wash your face, so that it will not be obvious to others that you are fasting, but only to your Father, who is unseen; and your Father, who sees what is done in secret, will reward you.
> —**Matthew 6:16-18**

Jesus taught us to fast with purpose. Before you fast, determine the purpose of your fast. Are you fasting in response to the Holy Spirit's leading? For spiritual breakthrough? To humble yourself? For breakthrough in others? Are you participating in a group fast called by spiritual leaders?

> Then John's disciples came and asked him, "How is it that we and the Pharisees fast often, but your disciples do not fast?" Jesus answered, "How can the guests of the bridegroom mourn while he is with them? The time will come when the bridegroom will be taken from them; then they will fast. —**Matthew 9:14-15**

Jesus taught us that there are spiritual issues that can only be resolved through prayer combined with fasting.

And when he was come into the house, his disciples asked him privately, Why could not we cast him out? And he said to them, This kind can come forth by nothing, but by prayer and fasting. —**Mark 9:28-29 AKJV**

HOW THE EARLY CHURCH VIEWED FASTING

The Apostles and the early church viewed fasting as a normal part of a believer's life. They particularly seemed to fast while seeking direction concerning significant decisions.

Paul was anointed for his life purpose after a time of fasting and prayer.

While they were worshiping the Lord and fasting, the Holy Spirit said, "Set apart for me Barnabas and Saul for the work to which I have called them." So after they had fasted and prayed, they placed their hands on them and sent them off. —**Acts 13:2-3**

The Church fasted while appointing leaders and seeking direction.

Paul and Barnabas appointed elders for them in each church and, with prayer and fasting, committed them to the Lord, in whom they had put their trust. —**Acts 14:23**

WHAT TO EXPECT WHEN YOU FAST

Expect some discomfort while fasting.

- You will typically experience hunger pains and "light-headedness."

- Fasting some foods, such as caffeine and sugar, can have a withdrawal effect, causing headaches and irritability. These symptoms should subside after a few days.

- You might experience weakness, so limit physical activity and get plenty of rest. Pay attention to your body. Consider medical attention if you experience extreme fatigue, persistent dizziness or fainting.

- You might encounter spiritual opposition while fasting.

(Remember this lesson is not intended for medical advice. It is general observations concerning Biblical fasting. Please contact your doctor with any medical questions.)

Expect spiritual benefit. Sometimes you won't sense a breakthrough while you're fasting. Hunger and irritability can often cloud your senses. The full spiritual impact will often not be felt until after the fast is over.

> No discipline seems pleasant at the time, but painful. Later on, however, it produces a harvest of righteousness and peace for those who have been trained by it. —**Hebrews 12:11**

LENGTH AND FREQUENCY OF FASTING

The length and frequency of fasting depends upon several factors. What is God leading you to do? Is it a total-food fast or a partial-food fast? Total-food fasts are typically for one to three days but can be longer. Partial-food fasts are typically for extended periods of time. Most (but not all) Biblical fasts were for one day.

Some people make it a practice to fast one day every week. The fast is not out of ritual, but rather to routinely keep themselves humbled in the Presence of God. Others only fast occasionally when they feel directed to do so by the Holy Spirit. Others will fast certain times of the year.

It was a common practice in Scripture for leaders to call a group fast. This applied to nations in the Old Testament and to the Church in the New Testament. Numerous Biblical accounts of fasting were a group endeavor.[14]

FASTING TIPS:

Fast sensibly. Most Biblical fasts were for one day, with few exceptions. For extended fasts, people often only abstained from certain foods or activities they enjoyed, rather than all food. Extended fasts are often engaged in by just eating one meal a day for a designated time.

Drink plenty of water. Keep your body hydrated while you fast.

Eliminate time-wasters while fasting. For example, turn off anything with a screen (TV, computer, game device, smart device). Use only if required for your work. Set a time twice a day to check for messages; other than that, set it aside.

In order to have spiritual benefit, fasting should be combined with prayer and Scripture reading. Pray and feed your mind and spirit on the Word of God. When you are hungry, read and study and pray. When you are weak, feed your spirit. When you are bored, feed your spirit.

Children should not go without eating. If a child wants to participate in a fast, perhaps they could give up a "favorite" food or give up a toy or an activity that they enjoy.

Before fasting, consult your doctor. This is especially important if you are on medication or have certain health issues. If you should not engage in a total-fast food because of medical reasons, consider an activities fast or a partial-food fast.

1. Have you ever engaged in a fast? If yes, what type and for how long?

2. What are your thoughts or questions concerning
    fasting?

3. Consider engaging in a fast. What type of fast will it be,
    and for how long?

corporate prayer

Developing a personal relationship with God is vital to your spiritual growth. Deep, personal times with God and hearing the Father's voice in your day-to-day life should be normal.

However, our relationship with God can often be so individual-ized that we are devoid of the power that comes only through praying with others—corporate prayer; this includes praying with believers from your home church congregation and also uniting with other congregations for prayer. Corporate prayer gatherings are not only a time to worship together (although prayer and worship often go hand-in-hand) nor are they a time to just hear teaching about prayer. We must actually gather and *pray*.

> For where two or three have gathered together
> in My name, I am there in their midst.
> —**Matthew 18:20 NASB**

It's important to realize that Christians do not have to agree on everything in order to pray together. We can even think our brother or sister is wrong about a theological issue, but if we agree about the Lordship of Jesus and are willing to express grace and Christian love for each other, then we can pray together.

EXAMPLES FROM SCRIPTURE

*   Jesus stated that two or three gathered in his name brings His Presence. (Matthew 18:20)

*   The Apostle James taught that when we confess our faults and pray for each other, we will receive healing. (James 5:16)

- The first church congregation gathered and remained in prayer until they received power. (Luke 24:49)

- The same church group met together and prayed for the Apostles when they were imprisoned. While the church prayed, God sent an angel to release them. (Acts 12:5-7)

- Paul and Silas prayed together in prison, and God released earth-shaking power that set them free. (Acts 16:25-26)

EXAMPLES FROM CHURCH HISTORY

Moravian Missions Movement: In the 1700s, Moravians were a group of Christians who lived communally, due to outside persecution. Division crept in, then corporate prayer was called. According to their account, the Holy Spirit was "poured out" on the entire assembly.

What ensued was a 100-year, 24-hour-every-day prayer meeting; subsequently hundreds from their group gave their lives to serve in world missions. Some credit this movement with producing the First Great Awakening in the Unites States. It was through the influence of the Moravians that John Wesley encountered the Holy Spirit of Jesus and became the great revivalist he is known to be.[15]

Fulton Street Prayer Revival: In 1857, God moved upon Rev. Jeremiah Lanphier to gather people to pray at noon on Fulton Street, New York. Within 18 months, similar prayer groups had formed in cities all over the United States an estimated 1 million people gave their life to Jesus—all through corporate prayer meetings.[16]

Cane Ridge Revival: From August 6-12, 1801, believers from Cane Ridge, Kentucky who attended different churches met together for prayer and communion, an annual three-to-five-day meeting ending with the Lord's Supper. Typically, people gathered in the dozens, maybe the hundreds. However, at this Cane Ridge Communion, as many as 20,000 people arrived.

What ensued was a revival that brought salvation to thousands of people. Vanderbilt historian Paul Conkin said it was "arguably… the most important religious gathering in all of American history."[17]

The Welsh Revival: Prayer gripped young, Welsh Evan Roberts and his spiritual companions in 1904. He attended a prayer meeting and asked those who were seeking for a deeper spiritual life to stay behind. Together they prayed and gave themselves to the cause of Christ; as a result, revival hit the entire island of Wales.

Tens of thousands were saved. The revival was a leading story in major newspapers. Lists of people who were converted were even printed in local town newspapers. Popular national sporting events were cancelled or postponed due to the impact of the revival on the nation. Bars and gambling establishments were shut down. Factories temporarily closed for day-time prayers, as public prayer meetings became a major vehicle for revival.[18]

Billy Graham Revivals: Twentieth Century Evangelist Billy Graham sent workers to organize prayer among local churches prior to conducting city-wide revivals, or crusades as he called them. Millions were saved through these gatherings over the course of his ministry; from 1947-2005, Billy Graham conducted 417 crusades in 185 countries and territories on six continents.[19]

These are just a few examples from church history that demonstrates the power of corporate prayer.

Should you have a personal relationship with God? Absolutely. Should you pray individually? Absolutely. Jesus gave us that example many times when He went off by Himself to pray. But He also taught us to pray together.

1. **In your church experiences, how much has corporate prayer been emphasized?**

2. From the examples of corporate prayer listed today, which stands out to you?

3. What is your commitment level to making corporate prayer a regular part of your life?

notes

God's intervention

God grant me the serenity to accept the things I cannot change, the courage to change the things I can, and the wisdom to know the difference. —PRAYER FOR SERENITY

involving God

We will now discuss the relationship between prayer and God's intervention in the world today.

Many times, when you pray, God intervenes. Other times it seems that He does not. People mark this up to *God's mysterious will*, but careful examination of Scripture shows there can be other factors at play.

We'll begin by exploring the fact that we often don't receive because we don't ask.

Some people are reluctant to ask for God's intervention because they don't want to appear to be using God or only asking Him for favors. Other people only talk to God when they want something.

It is true that you should not only talk to God when you need things; that isn't a relationship. However, if you regularly speak with Him, you should expect your needs to come up during the course of conversation. They are a natural part of your relationship.[20]

1. In what ways does allowing your requests to flow out of a natural relationship with God differ from talking to God only when you need something?

It's okay to ask for God's help within the context of your relationship with Him. Jesus taught that your Heavenly Father already knows what you need before you ask Him. Then He says, *"Ask."*

> Ask and it will be given to you; seek and you
> will find; knock and the door will be opened to
> you. For everyone who asks receives; the one
> who seeks finds; and to the one who knocks,
> the door will be opened. —**Matthew 7:7-8**

You may wonder, *Why doesn't God just do the "right" thing anyway? Why should I even have to ask Him?*

Our authority and responsibility. God gives you a good deal of authority to determine the outcome of things. The Bible is full of stories—beginning with the command to Adam and Eve to subdue and rule the earth—of things God could have done Himself, yet He gave or shared responsibility with humans.[21]

Prayer is simply the spiritual aspect of the authority God gave you. God ordains things in such a way that you can influence Him through prayer. Not because He needs you to, but because He wants *you.* Many times, He waits until you ask—until you invite Him into the situation—before He releases His Power into it.

Remember that a loving relationship is what God wants from you more than anything else. He wants your love, your will and your heart totally surrendered to Him. Many times, He limits His intervention until you get to the point of surrender and give it all to Him. He wants you to ask Him into your circumstances. Like any loving Father, He wants to hear you say, *"Dad, I need some help."* God is not a control freak. Often, He simply waits to be humbly invited in.

> But he gives us more grace. That is why
> Scripture says: "God opposes the proud but
> shows favor to the humble." —**James 4:6**

2. What is your reaction to the thought that God shares responsibility with people?

3. In which areas of your life have you failed to involve God and then wondered why He didn't intervene?

do an attitude check

Scripture teaches that God can actually desire something for you, but the condition of your heart and your attitude can block it.

The following verses explain how the condition of your heart can limit God's intervention in your life:

> When you ask, you do not receive, because you ask with wrong motives, that you may spend what you get on your pleasures. —**James 4:3**

1. **According to this verse, which heart condition can limit God's intervention in your life?**

2. **In what ways has selfish motivation influenced your prayer?**

It's your sins that have cut you off from God.
Because of your sins, he has turned away and
will not listen anymore. —**Isaiah 59:2 NLT**

3. **According to this verse, which heart condition can limit God's intervention in your life?**

4. **Which patterns of sin in your life may limit God's intervention in your life?**

Those who shut their ears to the cries of the
poor will be ignored in their own time of need.
—**Proverbs 21:13 NLT**

5. **According to this verse, which heart condition can limit God's intervention in your life?**

6. **What is your attitude toward others who are in need?**

But when you ask, you must believe and not
doubt, because the one who doubts is like
a wave of the sea, blown and tossed by the
wind. That person should not expect to receive
anything from the Lord. Such a person is
double-minded and unstable in all they do.
—James 1:6-8

7. **According to this verse, which heart condition can limit
God's intervention in your life?**

8. **In which areas do you waver in your request?**

It seems that sometimes God waits to see how serious you are about a request before He intervenes. If God said, *"Yes"* to everything you asked for, it would not be long before you would pray to counteract your previous requests.

Sometimes we need to wait. Also, realize there are times God may not be saying, *"No"* to a request. He may simply be telling you to wait.

- Sometimes you need to *grow up*—develop your character and abilities.

- Sometimes you need to *slow down*—the timing is wrong.[22]

9. **What is the difference between no and wait?**

do a responsibility check

Sometimes God will not intervene in a situation because you want *Him* to do what He expects *you* to do. Remember that He gave you a level of authority to carry out His will in the world. With that comes a certain amount of responsibility.

Sometimes you may wonder how to know the difference — *Is this my responsibility to handle, or is it God's?*

First learn what God's Word says about the subject. If you are still unclear, you should fire in the spiritual direction of prayer, and also fire in the physical direction of doing what you *can* do.

Here are some examples:

- If you are having marital problems, or problems with your teen, you should pray and take spiritual authority over the damage Satan is causing in your family. At the same time, you should take a step such as seeking counseling to learn new ways to communicate with each other.

- If you have a conflict with someone, you can pray that God will bring peace in the situation; but Scripture directs you to attempt to work it out—to approach the person one-on-one and later take a mediator if necessary (Matthew 18:15-17).

- If you need a job, you can pray and ask God to provide opportunities; but you need to take the initiative to do things such as polishing up your résumé or maybe learning new skills.

- If you are sick, you can pray and ask God to intervene and heal. But if your diet and habits are unhealthy, it is your responsibility to change them.

Remember the Serenity Prayer: *God grant me the serenity to accept (or release into Your hands) the things I cannot change, the courage to change the things I can, and the wisdom to know the difference.*[23]

1. **Which people/situations do you need to release to God because you cannot change them?**

2. **Which situations require a response from you, but you lack the courage to do what you need to do?**

Have I not commanded you? Be strong and courageous. Do not be afraid; do not be discouraged, for the LORD your God will be with you wherever you go. —**Joshua 1:9**

I am the vine; you are the branches. If you remain in me and I in you, you will bear much fruit; apart from me you can do nothing. —**John 15:5**

do a "free will" check

God has given people free will. This means that God gives people the choice to do the right thing or not.

> This day I call the heavens and the earth as witnesses against you that I have set before you life and death, blessings and curses. Now choose life, so that you and your children may live. —**Deuteronomy 30:19**

As you have already learned, what God desires most from you is a love-based relationship. True love can only be based on a choice. If someone is forced to love you, can that really be love?

In other words, in order for you to truly make a choice to love God, you must have the ability to choose to *not* love God. With every choice a person makes there is an option to choose wrong—to choose evil.[24]

Sometimes you may ask God to force someone to do the right thing. In doing this, you are praying for God to temporarily take away their free will. If God took away your free will every time you tried to do the wrong thing, would you really have free will?

You can ask God to speak to others' hearts and let them see clearly the decision they are making. If Satan is blinding them (2 Corinthians 4:4), you can take spiritual authority over his influence and ask God to bring clarity—but they still have to choose.

You can ask God to draw others' hearts to Him (John 6:44) or ask Him to send people into their lives to speak to them. But they still have the choice to accept or reject Him. He does not force you or others to follow Him.

1. **In what ways have you prayed that God would remove someone else's free will and force them to do the right thing?**

2. **Based on this lesson, how will your prayer focus for them change?**

SUFFERING FROM OTHER PEOPLE'S CHOICES

If someone is hurting you, you may not understand why God does not force them to stop. Remember that everyone has free will; we choose how to use it. Whichever level of good someone can do; they have the potential to do the same level of evil.

The Bible says that one day God will punish sin and destroy the wicked. Until that time, people choose what they do.

Say to them, "As surely as I live, declares the
Sovereign Lord, I take no pleasure in the death
of the wicked, but rather that they turn from
their ways and live. Turn! Turn from your evil
ways! Why will you die, people of Israel?"
—Ezekiel 33:11

CAUTION: If you are being physically and/or emotionally
harmed, you should take personal responsibility and choose to
remove yourself from the destructive situation if at all possible.

3. **In what ways have other people's choices brought pain into your life?**

do a consequence check

God often does not intervene because you ask Him to spare you or others from the consequences of decisions.

Let's do a review:

It is true that God promises forgiveness of sins and that Jesus bore the penalty of your sins. However, in order to receive that forgiveness, you must turn away from sin (repent) and surrender to Jesus' direction. You must choose to live with Jesus as the Lord of your life (Acts 2:38, Romans 10:9).

In other words, you cannot continue to do what you want and expect God to bail you out. You must learn how to make new decisions in order to have new outcomes. (This is closely related to the responsibility check we learned on *Day 14: Do a Responsibility Check).*

> Do not be deceived: God cannot be mocked.
> A man reaps what he sows. Whoever sows
> to please their flesh, from the flesh will reap
> destruction; whoever sows to please the Spirit,
> from the Spirit will reap eternal life.
> **—Galatians 6:7-8**

> What then? Shall we sin because we are not
> under the law but under grace? By no means!
> Don't you know that when you offer yourselves
> to someone as obedient slaves, you are slaves
> of the one you obey—whether you are slaves
> to sin, which leads to death, or to obedience,
> which leads to righteousness?
> **—Romans 6:15-16**

For example, if you keep abusing your relationships you will probably reap the harvest of a failed relationship. If you keep abusing your body through unhealthy eating or through drugs and alcohol you will probably reap poor health. If you keep committing crimes, you will probably go to jail.

Asking God to change the consequences will not help if you keep making wrong choices. The right prayer is to ask for God to give you the power to overcome the desires of your flesh that produce harmful consequences. (Reference *Workbook 2: Discover Freedom,* for more help with overcoming sinful desires and patterns).

1. According to the above verses, what is the result of continuing to obey your sin nature?

2. What is the result of obeying God's direction?

3. In which areas of your life do your actions continue to produce death, yet you keep asking God to "fix it" for you?

BEARING OTHER PEOPLE'S CONSEQUENCES — ARE YOU IN THE WAY?

With the ability to choose comes the consequences of your choices (Deuteronomy 30:19). Consequences are God's way of helping us to learn right from wrong.

Sometimes you absorb someone else's consequences and then wonder why they're not motivated to change. Why *should* they change? They do what they want while you pay the price for their choice. Or you fix their messes, rather than letting them learn from their mistakes.[25]

In other words, God is *trying* to shape them through consequences, but you are in the way. Rather than continuing to ask God to change them and being disappointed with God when they don't change, perhaps you should allow them to experience the consequences of their choices.

4. **In which areas/situations do you need to stop protecting someone from the consequences of their behavior?**

WILL GOD SPARE US FROM EARTHLY CONSEQUENCES OF OUR SIN?

It's possible for God, motivated by His mercy, to intervene in the consequences of bad choices. However, this is usually only in response to a truly changed, repentant heart —not just sorrow for getting caught. Remember, God is not in any way obligated to spare us the consequences of our decisions. He does not owe us.

It's not wrong to ask God to help you through consequences that you're suffering from past mistakes. But if God doesn't intervene, lean on Him for the strength to bear the repercussions and seek to grow from them.

Remember, God wants you to be saved and transformed. He's more interested in who you become than in your immediate comfort. It's better to bear temporary sufferings in this world and be changed by them than it is to be spared those sufferings and spend eternity separated from God.

> For I consider that the sufferings of this present time are not worthy to be compared with the glory that is to be revealed to us.
> —Romans 8:18 NASB

5. **What are your thoughts or questions concerning the value of consequences and the fact that God might not intervene to spare you from the results of bad choices?**

understanding spiritual opposition

If you've worked through all the other factors that limit God's intervention and you still haven't received an answer concerning your prayer, you might be experiencing spiritual opposition.

You have a real spiritual opponent in this world. Satan and other fallen angels have chosen to resist God and His will for humanity.

- Three times in the book of John (John 12:31, John 14:30 and John 16:11), Jesus calls Satan the prince of this world.

- In Ephesians 2:2, Apostle Paul calls him the ruler of the kingdom of the air.

- In 2 Corinthians 4:4, Apostle Paul calls him the god of this world (or the god of this age).

- In Ephesians 6:12, Apostle Paul says there are spiritual principalities and powers at work in the world, and we are to combat them through prayer.

The prophet Daniel prayed and waited 21 days for an answer. God sent an angel to deliver His response. Notice what the angel told Daniel:

> Then he continued, "Do not be afraid, Daniel. Since the first day that you set your mind to gain understanding and to humble yourself before your God, your words were heard, and I have come in response to them. But the prince

of the Persian kingdom resisted me twenty-one
days. Then Michael, one of the chief princes,
came to help me, because I was detained there
with the king of Persia." —**Daniel 10:12-13**

God heard Daniel as soon as he prayed, but the answer was spiritually opposed. When you humble yourself and pray, God hears you in that moment (Matthew 6:7). You do not have to say the same thing over and over to get God to listen, but the answer could be spiritually opposed. So, persistence with prayer could be necessary.

Notice this example in the New Testament: Paul said he could not go to the city of Thessalonica because Satan hindered him.

For we wanted to come to you—certainly I,
Paul, did, again and again—but Satan blocked
our way. —**1 Thessalonians 2:18**

Check through all the other things that you have learned that can delay God's intervention. If they are in order but God's intervention is still delayed, it could be the result of spiritual opposition.

If you believe that you are being spiritually opposed, continue praying and faithfully wait. Trust that God will bring victory on your behalf. God often uses these times to shape your character. Sometimes what really matters is not how long you wait, but *how* you wait.[26]

1. **In what ways does the idea of spiritual opposition differ from what you thought?**

CONCLUDING THOUGHTS ABOUT GOD'S INTERVENTION

When you think about the fact that people's free will *and* spiritual beings can interfere with God's purposes, it may give you the impression that God is weak. Understand that God will ultimately accomplish His purpose for humanity. People and Satan may delay or detour it, but they cannot defeat it. Just like water seeks lower ground, God's purposes seek completion. If you dam up moving water it will eventually flow over, around, or break through the obstacle.[27]

If this world is truly at war as Scripture describes, there will be many things that do not make sense. Some things may never be understood until you are face-to-face with God. Until that day, you must remain faithful with what you have—and continue to trust God. Trust that His will and purposes will be accomplished in the earth.

Be faithful. Do what you can with what you have. Each of us will answer for what has been entrusted to us.

Trust God. Know that your life is in His hands. No matter what happens, you'll be okay. Even if it means your death, you have eternity with Him to look forward to.

2. **Read Revelation 21:1-5 in your Bible. Write about the promises found there.**

Thank God for your future with Him and ask Him to help you remain faithful—and trust Him with your present.

studying scripture

Study to show yourself approved to God, a workman that needs not to be ashamed, rightly dividing the word of truth.

– 2 TIMOTHY 2:15 AKJV

the importance of scripture

The Holy Bible is the written Word of God. The word Bible comes from the word *biblia,* which means *books.*[28] The Bible is actually 66 books broken up into two sections: The Old and New Testaments. The Old Testament is made up of 39 books; the New Testament has 27.

The Bible was written over the span of thousands of years, by more than 40 writers with different backgrounds and styles. When you see their consistent theme and message, you see evidence of the Divine Author, God, expressing Himself through human writers.

> All Scripture is God-breathed and is useful for teaching, rebuking, correcting and training in righteousness, so that the servant of God may be thoroughly equipped for every good work.
> —II Timothy 3:16-17

The written Scriptures were given to provide at least four things to a believer:

- A Written Record

- Communication with God

- Spiritual Nourishment

- A Moral Code

A WRITTEN RECORD

The written Word provides a record of God's interactions with mankind. This helps us understand the scope of what God has been doing throughout history. We tend to only see current events and our own lives playing out in the world. By reading Scripture, we understand how God has been at work in the world throughout thousands of years. This helps us understand our role in God's big story.

We can trust that the Biblical record is both *reliable* and *valid*.[29]

To say the Bible is *reliable* means that what we read today is what the writers recorded. Because none of the original texts of the Bible exist, all translators use copies of the original texts. Some people insist that the texts have been so tampered with it is impossible to know what was written. Thorough scientific investigation disproves this claim.

Minor copying errors may be found from one manuscript to another, but these are easily caught by the trained eye. When manuscripts older than those used for our current translations of the Bible were discovered, examined and compared, very few copy errors were found. The evidence is strong that what we currently read is reliably close to what was originally written and intended.

To say the Bible is *valid* means that the Bible is true. It is what it claims to be, and its message can be trusted. Through the inspiration of God, the writers recounted incidents that they witnessed, and they gave instruction from God. In other words, they were not lying about what they wrote.

Some accuse Bible writers of not properly recording details, insisting that the books of the Bible were written too many years after their recorded events to be accurate and trustworthy. However, most of the recorded events in the Bible were recorded soon after they occurred.

Although several other, ancient, historical narratives were written hundreds of years after events transpired, some critics give these other narratives more historical weight than the accounts of Scripture that were written soon after their recorded events. This is a hypocritical standard.

People also accuse Biblical writers of a conspiracy to manipulate people. However, many of them died defending their claims. It's unlikely that so many people would be willing to die for something they *knew* was a lie.

1. **Do you trust that the Bible is both reliable and valid? Explain:**

2. **If not, what is your next step to address your doubt?**

COMMUNICATION WITH GOD

God desires to speak to us through Scripture. Because God is the Author of Scripture and has given Scripture to His people across time, He has an intended purpose for it that goes beyond any particular issues that were addressed when it was originally written. This means that Scripture has a *historical purpose* (what it meant to its original readers) and an *eternal importance* (including how it applies to our lives).[30] Learning how to engage with the Holy Spirit and discern His voice through studying the written Word of God—the Bible—is a vital component to your spiritual growth.

We have already learned that God can speak to us through His Spirit in prayer. This brings up important questions:

* How do you really know if God is speaking to you?

* How can you tell the difference between God's voice and the voice of culture or your own voice in your mind?

One of the best ways to recognize God's voice is by getting familiar with His written Word—the Bible. God inspired men to write the Word. Although the background, styles and vocabularies of human writers are reflected in Scripture, God is the divine Author who directed them.

> Above all, you must understand that no prophecy of Scripture came about by the prophet's own interpretation of things. For prophecy never had its origin in the human will, but prophets, though human, spoke from God as they were carried along by the Holy Spirit. —**2 Peter 1:20-21**

> But the Advocate, the Holy Spirit, whom the Father will send in my name, will teach you all things and will remind you of everything I have said to you. —**John 14:26**

> My sheep listen to my voice; I know them, and they follow me. —**John 10:27**

Because God is the Author of the written Word, He will not speak to you or guide you in a way that is contrary to what His Word teaches.

The more you read the words of Christ, the more discerningly you will recognize His voice in your heart. The more you read His teachings, you will begin to learn the *tone* and *character* of His voice. You will get a sense of what Jesus "sounds like."

3. Explain how reading the written Word can help you learn the tone and character of God's voice.

SPIRITUAL NOURISHMENT

In the same way that our physical bodies need food in order to grow and live, the child of God needs nourishment. Notice the following passages of Scripture teach us that God's Word is like food:

> How sweet are your words to my taste, sweeter than honey to my mouth! ——**Psalms 119:103**

> When your words came, I ate them; they were my joy and my heart's delight, for I bear your name, LORD God Almighty. ——**Jeremiah 15:16**

> Jesus answered, "It is written: 'Man shall not live on bread alone, but on every word that comes from the mouth of God.'" ——**Matthew 4:4**

> Like newborn babies, long for the pure milk of the word, so that by it you may grow in respect to salvation, if you have tasted the kindness of the Lord. ——**I Peter 2:2-3 NASB**

You may begin to notice a sense of peace and fulfillment as you begin to read and study Scripture. Many find it brings purpose and center to their day. This happens because your spirit receives nourishment from the Word of God.

4. What does it mean to say that your spirit needs nourishment?

5. Have you ever experienced a change in your mind or attitude as you read Scripture? Explain:

A MORAL CODE

Everyone has a different value system and opinions about what is right or wrong. Depending on the culture in which you were raised, some things that seem normal and right to you are actually destructive and need to change.

> There is a way that appears to be right, but in the end it leads to death. —**Proverbs 16:25**

As a Christian, you must go to God and find out what He says. You have submitted your life to Christ's Lordship, which means that you accept His standard for right and wrong. The Bible was given to us to show what God desires.

As a Christian, God's Word—not people's opinions, your culture or your family's traditions—must determine your moral compass. Scripture's purpose is to shape us into the character of Christ so that we can do the works God created us to do. (Reread II Timothy 3:16-17.)

Remember that the most important meaning of Scripture is the direction and change it brings in you. Bible Study for the sake of studying the Bible is ultimately useless. If Scripture is not shaping you and changing you into the image of Christ, then it has not served its intended purpose.

> For those God foreknew he also predestined to be conformed to the image of his Son, that he might be the firstborn among many brothers and sisters. —**Romans 8:29**

6. **In what ways can reading Scripture guide or change your behavior?**

BOOKS OF THE BIBLE

OLD TESTAMENT BOOKS - 39

Books of the Law - 5
Genesis
Exodus
Leviticus
Numbers
Deuteronomy

Books of History - 12
Joshua
Judges
Ruth
1 Samuel
2 Samuel
1 Kings
2 Kings
1 Chronicles
2 Chronicles
Ezra
Nehemiah
Esther

Books of Poetry - 5
Job
Psalms
Proverbs
Ecclesiastes
Song of Solomon

Books of Major Prophets - 5
Isaiah
Jeremiah
Lamentations
Ezekiel
Daniel

Books of Minor Prophets - 12
Hosea
Joel
Amos
Obadiah
Jonah
Micah
Nahum
Habakkuk
Zephaniah
Haggai
Zechariah
Malachi

NEW TESTAMENT BOOKS - 27

Gospels - 4
Matthew
Mark
Luke
John

History - 1
Acts

Paul's Letters to Churches - 9
Romans
1 Corinthians
2 Corinthians
Galatians
Ephesians
Philippians
Colossians
1 Thessalonians
2 Thessalonians

Paul's Letters to Friends - 4
1 Timothy
2 Timothy
Titus
Philemon

General Letters - 8
Hebrews
James
1 Peter
2 Peter
1 John
2 John
3 John
Jude

Letter and Prophecy-1
Revelation

translations

In order to allow God to speak to you through His Word, you must be able to understand what you are reading. The original languages of the Bible were Hebrew, Aramaic and Greek. These are all "dead" languages—no current culture communicates with them.

To read Biblical texts we must learn to read the original languages or rely upon scholars who have spent lifetimes studying the original languages and translating them for us. It can be more reliable to allow a scholar to translate for us than to take several years to learn the original languages and decipher the text ourselves.

Think of it this way: Who has a better understanding of medicine? A team of specialists who spent years studying their field of medicine and a lifetime practicing it, or a student with a medical dictionary? The student with the dictionary can certainly learn new things by consulting it, but their overall command of the field cannot match what a lifetime of experience offers.

UNDERSTANDING THE TYPES OF TRANSLATIONS

Translating languages can be tricky. Languages often have different grammatical structures, so it can be confusing to translate word for word. Some liberties must be taken by all translators to help the reader to better understand ideas being communicated by the text. Most translations fall on a continuum from *formal* through *functional* to *free*.[31]

Formal translations: Formal, or literal, translations try to follow the exact language as much as possible. Rearrangement of word order or sentence structure is done very little. The *King James Version,* the *English Standard Version* and the *New American Standard Bible* are examples of formal translation. The more formal the translation, the more word-for-word it is. This can present some problems with comprehension, as the flow and structure of grammar differs from language to language.

Functional translations: Functional translations focus more on conveying the idea of the original language. They are more likely to rephrase ideas and rearrange word order to make more sense in the new language. The *New International Version* is an example of a functional translation. Functional translations are more thought-for-thought than word-for-word.

Free translations: A free translation paraphrases the text. In other words, the translator or paraphraser restates the text in his or her own words. A paraphrase is good to read for a different perspective on a verse, but keep in mind it is strongly "flavored" with someone's opinion. *The Message* and *The Passion* translations are examples of free translation.

To study the Bible in earnest, formal *and* functional translations should be used.

THE BENEFIT OF COMPARING TRANSLATIONS

Because every translation has weaknesses and strengths, it's best to regularly use two or three versions when reading or studying. Ideally, this will include a combination of formal and functional. By doing this, you can capture and benefit from the translation experience of more scholars.[32]

It's helpful to pick one translation for your regular reading. This will allow you to memorize passages more easily and learn your way around Scripture. When seeking deeper understanding about a passage, it's a good idea to reference two or three other translations.[33]

Online resources including, BibleGateway.com and YouVersion.com, provide free access to multiple translations as well as study resources, reading plans, and apps to keep you on track.

1. **What are advantages and disadvantages of each translation style?**

   Formal:

   Functional:

   Free:

2. **What are the advantages of comparing several, valid translations?**

understanding biblical context

A key to understanding the meaning of Scripture is to learn how the books are laid out and understand where each one fits within the overall theme and story of the Bible. This is referred to as reading within Biblical context.

THE LAYOUT OF THE BOOKS OF THE BIBLE

As noted before, the word Bible comes from the word *biblia*, which means *books*. The Bible is actually 66 books broken up into two sections. The Old Testament is made up of 39 books; the New Testament has 27.

Not all books are arranged in chronological order. Some books were written by people who are introduced in a separate book. For example, Apostle Paul is introduced in the book of Acts, but he wrote several of the other New Testament books.

Some books give historical narratives from different accounts. For example, 1 Samuel and 2 Samuel, 1 Kings and 2 Kings, and 1 Chronicles and 2 Chronicles report many of the same historical stories from different peoples' accounts. The books of Matthew, Mark, Luke and John are four accounts of Jesus' life told from different perspectives.

NOTE: Memorizing the names of the books of the Bible in order will help you grasp how the entire Bible is laid out and which books are in each section. Consider doing this with your family. (Reference the Books of the Bible List on page 89.)

In order to understand Biblical context, it is helpful to understand the Bible's overarching story.

THE OVERARCHING BIBLICAL STORY

When we look at the story of Scripture, we see God's desire to have a family with whom to share eternity. The Bible explains mankind's original created state, the fall of man and God's work to redeem humanity back to Himself, and our intended purpose as His children.

As we read through the entire Bible, we see that God has dealt with mankind incrementally throughout history. He has communicated with us in ways we can understand. Each increment is like a step, each building on the previous, leading us toward Jesus Christ.

Hebrew Scriptures (Old Testament) point to Jesus. The Old Testament details the origin of the world, mankind's fall away from God, and God's Covenant with the nation of Israel. The Old Testament led mankind to the "fullness of time" when God as Jesus came to live on earth. The Law and the Prophets of the Old Testament were a foreshadowing of Jesus. They prepared people for the Kingdom of God to be given back to man through Him.

New Testament letters point back to Jesus. Many books of the New Testament were letters written by the Apostles to various churches. In them we see Jesus' first disciples living out His message through the power of His Spirit. Though they were living out His message through His power, they still had their fair share of problems and misunderstandings. The letters were written to teach truth and give direction to the family of God–the Church. Among other things, the Apostle's writings applied Jesus' teachings. They also explained how the Levitical Law of the Old Testament was fulfilled and addressed issues of Godly morality that non-Jewish Christians were unaware of.

Jesus is the center of it all. Beginning with the Gospels and continuing through the other books of the New Testament, we see that Jesus came to reconcile the world back to God—to make all things new. He is the exact representation of God—the visible image of an invisible God—so He has most clearly revealed God's character to us.

> But in these last days he has spoken to us by his
> Son, whom he appointed heir of all things, and
> through whom also he made the universe. The
> Son is the radiance of God's glory and the exact
> representation of his being, sustaining all things
> by his powerful word. —**Hebrews 1:2-3a**

The *will of God* is defined throughout Christ's life and teachings.
Through His death and resurrection, all things necessary for
our *salvation and reunion* with God are fulfilled. Through giving
us His Holy Spirit, everything we need to *live in God's will* is
made available.

Jesus' life and teachings as found in the Gospels are the example
of what a spiritually reborn son or daughter of God looks like.
God is in the process of conforming all re-born believers into this
image. (For more teaching on this, reference back to *Workbook 1:
Discover Identity, Day 12: The Importance of Jesus' Life and Teachings.*)

> For those God foreknew he also predestined to
> be conformed to the image of his Son, that he
> might be the firstborn among many brothers
> and sisters. —**Romans 8:29**

This does not mean that other Scriptures are less inspired or true
than Jesus' words. After all, it was the Spirit of Jesus—the Holy
Spirit—that spoke through the Prophets. It simply means that
Jesus has most clearly communicated God's desires for us. The
Father even spoke to the disciples and told them to listen to Jesus.

> While he was still speaking, a bright cloud
> covered them, and a voice from the cloud said,
> "This is my Son, whom I love; with him I am
> well pleased. Listen to him!" —**Matthew 17:5**

1. Explain how Jesus is the center of Scripture.

2. What does it mean to say the will of God is expressed through Christ's teachings?

3. Reference back to *Workbook 1: Discover Identity, Day 12: The Importance of Jesus' Life and Teachings.* List additional ideas concerning the importance of the life and teachings of Jesus.

understanding literary context

Literary context means that a Bible verse can best be grasped by understanding the complete passage that contains it. Ask yourself: *"What is the point of this passage?"* and, *"What is going on or what is being addressed?"*

It is important to understand that the Bible was *not* written in verses and chapters. Most books of the Bible are long and contain many ideas. Verses and chapters were added to help readers find their way around.

Remember the chapter and verse locations are manmade. Verses and chapters are helpful for reference purposes but be aware that one single verse usually doesn't contain the full idea being communicated. Also be aware that chapter breaks were sometimes placed in the middle of thoughts and ideas. The beginning of a next verse or chapter does not necessarily signify the start of a new idea.[34]

One of the easiest ways to get a false understanding of a passage is by randomly choosing and reading verses. You would never expect to understand another book or letter by just selecting random sentences—so why would you approach Scripture that way? You should be careful not to build beliefs by reading verses without understanding their full literary context.

Remember, the sentences around a sentence can *change* its meaning. For example: a sentence can state an idea, but then the next sentence can refute it by showing how it is wrong. If you read the sentence by itself, you will form a wrong conclusion.[35]

It's okay to reference a verse to support a belief (this study does this), as long as you accurately use the verse in context. You must make sure the verse actually means—in context—what you say it means.

1. List an example of how sentences around a sentence can change its meaning.

An example of taking a verse out of context: A common passage taken out of context is Jesus' instruction in Matthew 7:1-4 not to judge others. Some people read this passage and assume from it that people can never call an action sin, even if Scripture says it is. Others incorrectly assume that we must accept that all who say they are Christians are actually Christians, no matter what their actions and lives indicate.

When you read the *rest* of Jesus' teaching on the subject in Matthew 7:15-23, you find that Jesus actually taught the opposite of those things.

It is true that Jesus taught against elevating yourself by condemning others. He also taught that we can tell if a person is truly His by their actions. He said many confess Him as Lord with their mouths, but He has never known them. He even warned us to be careful of deceivers and "wolves in sheep's clothing." He taught that we can tell the real from the fake by their actions.

Common misconceptions of these verses illustrate the importance of reading the rest of the passages, thoughts and/or ideas before forming a belief about an isolated portion.

2. Explain the importance of understanding the meaning of a verse by reading it within the context of the verses surrounding it.

THE IMPORTANCE OF GENRE AND WRITING STYLE

Literary context also refers to the genre or style of writing. The books of the Bible are not all the same genre and weren't written in the same style or genre. Discovering the genre of the passage can make it easier to understand its meaning. (Reference the Books of the Bible List on page 89).

Many ask about what is literal or symbolic in Scripture. The genre and passage itself will typically indicate whether it is literal, symbolic, or exaggerated language in order to make a point.[36]

Historical narratives: These are to be read as fairly straightforward accounts of events that happened. However, when reading understand that ancient historians/scribes were more interested in recording the "Big Event" that was going on rather than recording every tiny detail.

The Gospels and the Book of Acts can also be referred to as historical accounts because they re-tell the life of Jesus and the beginning of the early church. This means that the recorded events and miracles in these books are not figurative; they really happened and the writers wrote about them as they were witnessed or told.

The Law: Some Old Testament books detailed the Law of Moses and the Old Covenant (agreement) between God and man. The Law directed every aspect of the nation of Israel's life. This included dietary, health and sanitation laws; civil and criminal laws; separation laws that governed the uniqueness of the nation of Israel in relation to other nations; religious, temple and ceremonial laws; and the morality code for God's people.

Poetry or wisdom literature: Reading poetry is very different from reading historical accounts. Its purpose is generally different, and it is written in a different style. Writers use colorful, symbolic language when constructing poetry and songs. For example, David's couch was not really swimming with tears (Psalms 6:6)

Prophetic books: In the Old Testament, God sent prophets to call people back to their Covenant with Him. They reminded people about the blessing of keeping the Covenant and curses that come by breaking it—and urged repentance. Most future "foretelling" that prophets performed was about the immediate future for the people they addressed based upon whether or not they turned back to God.

Many prophets recounted visions they saw and wrote in a style that has become known as Apocalyptical writing. This type of writing is symbolic and cannot be taken as literal. The text often indicates that the prophet was seeing a vision and writing his best description using what he knew. This is usually indicative of symbolic writing.

Letters: Most New Testament books were written as letters. Letters are designed to be read all the way through. Failure to do so can change or alter their meaning. The New Testament letters were often written in response to other letters, or to address issues reported to the writer. We only have the response of the Apostle and don't always have a clear picture of the issues being dealt with. This is similar to hearing only one side of a phone conversation. Understanding cultural and historical context can help shed light on the issues or problems being addressed in these letters.

3. Explain how knowing the writing style and genre of a book can help you better understand its meaning.

understanding historical and cultural context

When we read the Bible as Christian Scripture, we understand that its original intended audience is all of God's people throughout history. We simply read it at different times. Human writers may not have realized the scope of their audience, but the Author—God—did.[37]

Numerous Biblical scholars have pointed out this truth: We read the Bible with an acknowledgement that the texts were written at a particular point in time, initially addressed to a specific group of people in response to a particular need. However, we believe that God used these situations to give answers and instructions to *all* of His people throughout the ages. We understand that God has given *timeless importance* to Scripture for all of us.

The Holy Spirit can use a passage to communicate a specific, *personal* truth to you that initially communicated truth to its first readers. The key word is *truth*. If both applications of the passage are true, the current application cannot mean something contrary to its meaning for the original audience. It may have a *different application*, but not a *contrary meaning*.[38]

For example: You might not be experiencing King David's challenges, but the truth of his prayers and the promises of God revealed in his prayers can speak truth to your situation. You may not face the types of battles the nation of Israel faced in the Old Testament, but you can trust that obedience to God and faithfulness to His Word can produce victory over your own spiritual enemies.

1. What does it mean to say that God can apply a passage to your life in a manner that is different from, but not contrary to, the intended application for its first audience?

THE IMPORTANCE OF HISTORICAL AND CULTURAL CONTEXT

To understand what God is saying to you through Scripture, it helps to understand what He said to the original readers. To do this accurately, it helps to have a grasp of the historical and cultural context of the passage.

Historical and cultural context is similar to the setting of a story. It includes, but is not limited to, understanding the ancient world of the Bible. Understanding places, cultures and customs are all keys to historical context.

Knowing the background of the writer, the genre of the text, and what prompted the writing of the text to original readers also contributes to understanding historical context.

Although this can be difficult because we are separated by thousands of years of culture, the text itself can help us understand its historical context. Does the text reveal who is speaking? The audience being addressed? The setting of that particular Scripture?[39]

BIBLE STUDY TOOLS

When the text does not provide adequate information, Bible encyclopedias, Bible commentaries, and dictionaries are useful.

Concordance: A Bible concordance contains an alphabetical index of certain words and main references used in the Bible and also where the word or reference occurs. An "exhaustive" concordance features all of the words in the Bible.

Bible Encyclopedia: This tool contains definitions and articles about scores of words and terms used in Scripture. Most encyclopedias give full historical references such as date, environment, family life, customs, language, and literature.

Bible Atlas: A Bible atlas contains the geography, civilizations and cartography of the Holy Land in various phases throughout centuries. It also describes the movements of Biblical characters, trade routes and battles.

Bible Dictionary: A Bible dictionary contains entries related to the Bible, mostly concerning people, places, customs, events in Scripture, and doctrine.

Bible Commentary: A Bible commentary is someone's explanation and application of Scripture. They are often written by Bible scholars and theologians. A commentary is not the final word on the explanation of a verse but can shed light as you attempt to understand Scripture.

Lexicon: Bible lexicons provide definitions and meanings for original–New Testament Greek and Old Testament Hebrew–ancient languages to bring understanding about the origins and root meaning behind words. It also gives context and cultural meaning intended by the writers.

STUDYING ACCURATE SOURCES

Simply perusing the Internet for information is dangerous. Anyone with an opinion about anything can post something as "truth" without providing any valid reason or sources for their conclusions. The amount of inaccurate information that passes as "historical meaning" of the Bible—even by those who have degrees—is staggering.

Before you rely upon a person's work, make sure that it's from valid, reliable sources. Guard against thoughts such as, *Some other Pastor said it, therefore it must be true.* Most people don't intentionally lie; they just repeat what someone else, whom they trusted, told them—without checking sources.

2. What are some ways to make sure you are learning from valid, accurate sources?

THE IMPORTANCE OF A SINCERE HEART

The risk of wrong interpretation shouldn't cause us to live in fear of getting it wrong. It should motivate us to engage in proper study and do our best to correctly understand the context of Scripture and recognize the voice of God.

Trust that when you seek Him with a sincere heart and complete your due diligence; you'll be rewarded with finding Him.

> And without faith it is impossible to please God, because anyone who comes to him must believe that he exists and that he rewards those who earnestly seek him. —**Hebrews 11:6**

3. Do you believe that if you sincerely seek God, He will lead you into His truth?

applying historical and cultural context

Following are examples that demonstrate the ways in which historical and cultural context can help you better understand Scripture.

UNDERSTANDING GOD'S ACTIONS

Shaping your life into Christ's character and helping you understand God's voice and nature are the primary reasons that Scripture was given. Understanding the historical context of Scripture can be very important to help you understand the character and actions of God. Context can change the meaning of anything.

For example, when you read about the severity of God's actions throughout the Old Testament within the context of brutality and the hard-heartedness of the people of that time, you begin to realize that God had to take a harsh tone to deal with the ruthless people with whom He was seeking to communicate. God's nature is not harsh; but He spoke in ways that barbaric cultures would understand. When less severe messages were *received and understood*, God did not speak harshly.

If a misunderstanding of historical context clouds our interpretation of Scripture, then we are more likely to misunderstand God's intent, voice and nature. If we cannot discern the tone and "spirit" of God's true voice in Scripture, our interpretation will shape us into something other than what God intends.

1. Respond to the idea that if we do not properly discern God's intent in Scripture, our misunderstanding could shape us into something other than what God intends.

UNDERSTANDING "STRANGE" SCRIPTURAL COMMANDS

When you read Scripture, you will often encounter a command that seems odd or strange. You need to understand that God always has a reason for His commands.

For example, many laws in the Old Testament seem strange to us. One in particular is a command to carry a small shovel or stick in order to bury bodily waste (Deuteronomy 23:13).

This rule seems odd in today's world with sewage and sanitation systems. But when that command was given several thousand years ago, it was highly applicable. In a world that did not understand germs, bacteria and disease in the ways we do today, it's likely that communities and camps were extremely unsanitary and perfect breeding grounds for diseases. This command to bury bodily waste was brilliant—and predated science by several thousand years. Understanding cultural and historical context sheds new light on commands such as this.

Some Scriptures in the New Testament can also seem strange. Consider Paul's command to greet each other with a holy kiss. In many of today's cultures, this would be very odd and even offensive. Learning more about cultural context helps you understand that a brief kiss was a customary friendly greeting, similar to modern handshakes or fist bumps.

2. List some "strange" laws or requests, if any, that you have read in the Bible. Is this law or request still binding to a Christian? Why or why not?

CLARITY WHEN INSTRUCTIONS APPEAR TO "CONFLICT"

If Scripture seems to give conflicting instructions on a matter, both instructions are right. Context usually helps us better understand and clarify perceived differences. Some matters addressed in the early Church were reactions to specific, cultural issues and were not meant to be specific commands for all times or in every situation. Thus, the instructions differed or varied with context.

Key questions to consider are:

- Were there different instructions given on the topic?

- What is the final word given on the topic?

This is not to say that we can claim exemption from every New Testament command that we do not like by appealing to historical and cultural context. However, when there seems to be conflicting commands, historical and cultural context can shed light. We will learn more about how to apply every part of Scripture on *Day 26: Rejecting God's Word*.

   3. **List any perceived conflicting requests, if any, that you have read in the New Testament. What is the final conclusion on the subject?**

When in doubt, ask a Pastor or mature Christian to help you understand more about strange or conflicting commands found in Scripture.

applying old testament scripture

In the sense that there is just one people of God throughout all ages, the Old Testament is our Scripture as well. It is part of our heritage and our history; it tells the story of "our people."[40]

But an understanding of the entire Bible reveals that there is a New Covenant in place that supersedes the Old. This does not mean that the Old Covenant/Testament is irrelevant. It does mean that we need to seek New Covenant/Testament guidance in the application of Old Testament Scripture.

Because the teachings of Christ are the final words of God about a Christian's life and behavior (Hebrews 1:1-2), it's important for a Christian to understand what Jesus and the Apostles taught on any given matter.

1. **Why should we seek the teachings of Jesus and the Apostles on a matter first?**

UNDERSTANDING THE LEVITICAL LAW

The main questions people have with the Old Testament usually involve application of the Levitical Law. This is often called the Law of Moses and can be found in Exodus, Leviticus, Numbers and Deuteronomy. This Law was given to the nation of Israel. It dictated their life and practices as a nation. God gave the nation of Israel His Law to teach them how to live as His People in relation to God, each other and other nations.

To discover which parts of the Levitical Law are still applicable and viable today, it is best to defer to the teachings of New Testament writers. (Review *Day 23: Applying Historical and Cultural Context*). Remember that not everything in the Old Testament was part of the Levitical Law—and not all parts of the Levitical Law were cancelled. Learning the different classifications of the Levitical Law will help with understanding the Law's purpose and intent.

PARTS OF THE LEVITICAL LAW:

Dietary, health and sanitation laws: Although some of these laws might still be useful, they are not mandated for the New Testament believer. (We'll talk more about the usefulness of Old Testament Scripture later today).

Civil and criminal laws related to governing the physical nation of Israel: Because God was working to establish a physical nation—a people—through which He would bring His Son, these laws were necessary for Israel. God needed to set up a civil and criminal code to guide His people. The New Covenant focuses upon Jesus' Kingdom, which doesn't have geographical borders and isn't based in a particular country.

Separation laws that governed Israel's uniqueness in relation to other nations: As God was establishing a physical nation—a people—through whom He could bring His Son, He desired that they be distinct from the other nations around them and from the idol "gods" of this world.

These laws are not mandated in the New Covenant. The distinction of Jesus' Kingdom is the manifestation of His Lordship and character through the attitudes, actions and lives of His followers.

Temple and Ceremonial laws: These laws were in place to make things right between God and people. All of these laws were fulfilled through Jesus' death and resurrection.

God's moral code: The moral code was given to direct how we were to relate to God and people. This is reflected, but not contained exclusively, in the Ten Commandments (Exodus 20:1-17). The moral code of the Law was emphasized in the Apostles' teachings and was taken to a new level through Jesus.[41]

2. How does this agree with or differ from your understanding of the Levitical Law?

MORE ABOUT THE MORAL CODE OF GOD

In the Levitical Law, we see God working with humanity in its context. God's character and favor shine through, shaping the hearts of a Godless, barbaric society.

When we read the Law in context with all of Scripture, we see an incremental imparting of God's moral code. It begins with the Law and is taken to a higher level by Jesus. The next step does not destroy the previous but builds upon it.

For example: The Law states an *eye for an eye* (Exodus 21:24). Based on this, some accuse God of approving revenge. In light of the entirety of Scripture, a better interpretation is that God *limits* the scope of revenge. In a world governed by self-centered, hierarchical morals and laws, God commanded that the *maximum* restitution anyone could take was what was done to them. In other words, you could not kill someone for taking out your eye. You could only have their eye, not take their life. Centuries later, Jesus took this further. He built upon God's command to not take more than was taken from you. More importantly, He taught that there is freedom that comes through choosing to forgive rather than seek revenge (Matthew 5:17-48).

Jesus and the Apostles resolved issues of the Law while taking the moral code—which is how one treats God and others—to another level. They taught that it was not just actions that mattered, but the intent and desires of the heart.

3. **Explain how Jesus and the Apostles took the Moral Code of the Old Testament to a new level.**

THE USEFULNESS OF ALL SCRIPTURE

Not all of Scripture is directly related to soul salvation; but it all has use.[42]

> All Scripture is God-breathed and is useful for teaching, rebuking, correcting and training in righteousness, so that the servant of God[a] may be thoroughly equipped for every good work. —2 Timothy 3:16-17

The Law — Consider the usefulness of sanitation and health requirements of the Law. Hand-washing, quarantine for people with communicable diseases, and burying fecal matter were all useful regulations that God gave thousands of years before science discovered the benefits. These are not binding instructions for salvation or life in the Kingdom of God under the New Covenant—but they're still useful.

Historical Narratives — Historical narratives in the Old Testament show us how God has interacted with humanity from the beginning, where He is leading humanity, and the Spirit by which He leads us.

Prophets — Along with other things to come, many prophets foretold Jesus. The Prophets were also mediators of God's Covenant. They called people back to the tenets of the original Covenant, reminding them of the blessings and curses associated with their decisions and actions.

Wisdom Literature — Wisdom literature consists of prayers, reflections and wise advice. There is great value in using Psalms as prayers. There is useful advice in Proverbs. Ecclesiastes reflects on the meaning of life.

4. **What are your thoughts concerning the usefulness of Scripture that does not pertain to soul salvation?**

the role of other christians in bible study

We will explore the importance of Christian relations in further detail in *Workbook 4: Discover Relationships,* but it merits mention here. Other Christians can help us understand and apply God's Word to our lives. God uses other believers to help communicate His truth to us.[43]

Jesus taught that He is present in a unique way when the Church family gathers in His name.

> For where two or three gather in my name, there am I with them. —**Matthew 18:20**

This is why you need to take time to engage with God through His family—the Church—by participating in corporate worship services as well as personal Bible discussion and prayer with others.

It is recommended that you connect and become involved with one Church family. This ensures consistent spiritual direction, and limits confusion that may result from hearing differing doctrines. This also helps build stronger relationships and enables growth under the leadership of a Godly Pastor.

1. Had you previously believed God engages with us through others? What are your thoughts about this?

God speaks through our discussing Scripture with others.
Most New Testament Scriptures are letters that were sent to groups of Christians in various places. The letters were received and read to the entire group and then discussed.

2. **What are benefits of discussing Scripture with others rather than only studying alone?**

God speaks through the teaching of Pastors and leaders.
God placed Pastors and leaders in the church to provide oversight and leadership and to explain Scripture. These are essential elements to your spiritual growth and should be reasons to motivate you to connect to a spiritual family.

> So Christ himself gave the apostles, the prophets, the evangelists, the pastors and teachers, to equip his people for works of service, so that the body of Christ may be built up until we all reach unity in the faith and in the knowledge of the Son of God and become mature, attaining to the whole measure of the fullness of Christ. —**Ephesians 4:11-13**

The primary purpose of a sermon / message from your Pastors:

- Is *not* to merely create an exciting or inspirational event

- Is *not* to attempt to impress people with their speaking ability

- Is *not* to please people by repeating only things with which they agree

The purpose of teaching and preaching is to instruct and teach God's Word so that Christians will mature and grow. Godly leaders will challenge you to change and grow into Christ-likeness. They should also explain the *why* and *how* of the change they are teaching.

If a leader is teaching the truth of Scripture, you might not always like what you hear. You have to choose to conform to Scriptural truth rather than just seek out a preacher or teacher who tells you what you like or want to hear.

> For the time will come when people will not
> put up with sound doctrine. Instead, to suit
> their own desires, they will gather around them
> a great number of teachers to say what their
> itching ears want to hear. —II Timothy 4:3

If messages/sermons are meant to help you mature in Christ, you should take notes about what is taught while you listen. If you only listen to teaching, you will likely forget. If you don't put what you hear into practice, it's of no use. If you take notes, you can review your notes later and compare them against Scripture to verify the truth of what is being taught, and then seek ways to apply the truth you learned to your life.

> Do not merely listen to the word, and so
> deceive yourselves. Do what it says.
> —James 1:22

3. **In what ways does this differ from what you believed about the purpose of preaching and teaching?**

4. **What can you do to better remember and apply messages taught by Pastors?**

God speaks through church history. It is beneficial to remember that we have a long, rich history of Christian thinkers and teachers to draw from. Discovering how the Church has approached an issue or doctrine throughout history can answer many questions for us today. It can be particularly helpful to consult the writings of the church leaders of the first three centuries, because they were not far removed in time from Jesus and the Apostles.

5. **What are some benefits in consulting Church History when seeking to understand Scripture?**

NOTE: Make sure that what is spoken to you through others is in agreement with the written Word of God. Remember that the Holy Spirit will remind you of what Jesus has already taught in His Word. He will never direct you in any way that contradicts His written Word.

> But the Advocate, the Holy Spirit, whom the Father will send in my name, will teach you all things and will remind you of everything I have said to you. —**John 14:26**

how to study scripture

We have learned many useful things to help with understanding and applying Scripture to our lives. This lesson will help pull all of this together and can serve as a guide for your daily Bible Study. Make sure you tag this page and reference back to it as needed.

GETTING STARTED

Select a book. Bible study begins by selecting one book in the Bible and reading through it in small sections. It is important to read through the entire book you have chosen and not just skip around.

Remember that the Bible was not originally written in verses and chapters; scholars added these later to make it easier to find passages. The end of a verse or chapter does not necessarily indicate the end of a thought or an idea. If you do not read the entire book, you will miss the context of passages and are likely to form wrong conclusions about their meanings. In the same way that you read every sentence of a letter that someone sent you in order to understand what they wanted to say, don't skip around to read random verses.

Suggestions about which books to begin with. If you are not sure where to start, begin with any of the Gospels—Matthew, Mark, Luke or John. The Gospels are detailed accounts of Jesus' life and teachings. Then, with a good understanding of how Jesus lived and what He taught, move on to Acts which describes the beginning of the Christian Church. Next, keep working through the rest of the books of the New Testament, which are actual letters written to early Christians and churches. It is best to have a good knowledge of the New Testament *before* you begin to study the Old Testament.

Conduct background research. Spend time researching and understanding the genre, and the Biblical, historical and literary contexts before you begin reading a book of the Bible. Ask the following: *Who is speaking? Whom are they addressing? What is the setting?* [44]

1. Which book of the Bible will you study next? Why?

THE "I.D. METHOD" OF BIBLE STUDY

As we have already learned, Scripture was written to a specific group of people in a particular place and time. It is also true that Scripture was written to *all* of God's people for all time. This means that God wants to speak to you personally and give personal direction while you read Scripture—*it is important to involve Him.*

If you study Scripture without inviting the Holy Spirit—the Spirit of Christ—into the process and without listening intently to what He says, your time studying will not be productive. When you involve Him, He makes the Bible clear to you. You will not just gain simple knowledge; Scripture will come alive in your heart and change you. Notice what Jesus said to the religious scholars of His day:

> You study the Scriptures diligently because you think that in them you have eternal life. These are the very Scriptures that testify about me, yet you refuse to come to me to have life.
> —John 5:39-40

If you ask Jesus to identify His voice in the passage, He will help *illuminate*—bring to light—the meaning of the passage, and He will also give you *direction* from the passage. We refer to this as the *I.D. Method of Bible Study.*

Illumination: First ask the Holy Spirit to help you understand the meaning of the passage. Pause and think about the segment rather than just skim through it. Do not hurry. It's okay to work through just a few verses, or even a single verse, in one sitting. You may have to go back and reread the same passage repeatedly for several days.

As we've learned, understanding the genre and the Biblical, historical and literary contexts of the passage will help you interpret its meaning. Discussing passages of Scripture with others and listening to your Pastor's teaching will help clarify parts of Scripture that are unclear to you. But these activities are not enough.

Interpreting Scripture is not only a natural process, it is a spiritual process. When you read the Bible, expect the Holy Spirit to help you understand what you are reading. This is critical; many people don't expect guidance from the Spirit. (Reread John 5:39-40) Notice what the Holy Spirit is "highlighting" to you as you read.

2. **What differences do you expect from asking the Holy Spirit to illuminate Scripture as you read it?**

Direction: Now ask the Holy Spirit to direct your action based upon what you learned in the Scriptures. Remember that learning without action is useless. Prayerfully ask the following questions after reading a passage:[45]

1. Is there an attitude or belief I need to *change?*

2. Is there behavior I need to *stop* or one I need to *start?*

3. Is there a promise to *depend* upon?

4. Is there an idea or message I need to *share* with someone else?

There are many different things the Holy Spirit may prompt you to do as a result of reading God's Word. You should respond. Always remember that He will not ask you to do something that contradicts the rest of written Scripture. This is why a clear understanding of the *entire* Bible is important. If you are uncertain about a direction given to you during your prayer and Bible reading, discuss it with a Pastor or mature Christian.

Now let's practice what we've learned:

ACTION STEP:

Turn to Matthew 6:25-34 and read it carefully.

1. Conduct background research on the passage.

- *Who is speaking?*

- *Whom are they addressing?*

2. Prayerfully seek *Illumination* and *Direction* from the Holy Spirit. Write down what the Holy Spirit speaks to you while you pray and read. Be prepared to share these thoughts with other members in your study group.

- ***Illumination:*** *What is the Holy Spirit "highlighting" to me as I read this passage?*

- ***Direction:*** *What should I do in response to this reading? (Reference the four Direction questions listed above)*

DAY 27

rejecting God's Word

Read Mark 4:3-25 in your Bible

In this passage, Jesus taught that if God brings something to light in your life, you shouldn't hide from it. What is the point of turning on a light if you're just going to cover it up with darkness? When God's Word challenges you to change, you must submit to Him.

We have learned some valuable tools to help us understand and interpret Scripture. But remember this critical truth: Understanding and interpreting Scripture is only half the job of studying Scripture! *You must seek God's direction from what you read—and then act on it.*

1. **In what ways is ignoring God's Word like hiding a light?**

In the rest of this passage, Jesus taught the Parable of the Sower, which reveals several responses to hearing God's Word.

Hard Ground: You reject the Word

Rocky Ground: You accept the Word but quit following when it becomes difficult.

Thorny Ground: You accept the Word but allow it to be choked out by the worries and busyness of life.

Good Ground: You consistently apply the Word of God to your life.

HARD GROUND: REJECTING GOD'S WORD

> Some people are like seed along the path, where the word is sown. As soon as they hear it, Satan comes and takes away the word that was sown in them. —**Mark 4:15**

The first response is that of hard ground. The seed of God's Word is rejected and doesn't take root. Rejection of Scriptural truth is when you harden your heart and refuse to apply it. When you engage with Scripture and then make up reasons why it doesn't apply to you, you're rejecting God's Word.

> Today, if you hear his voice, do not harden your hearts. —**Hebrews 4:7b**

The comfort filter approach: Too often we apply a "comfort filter" when it comes to applying Scripture to our lives: *Is this something I'm comfortable doing? Is this something I want to do?*

We might even dismiss a difficult teaching of Jesus with, *"He couldn't have meant that!"* because it's difficult or makes us uncomfortable. In other words, we obey if we want to. If we don't want to, we look for an "out" or simply ignore it.

It is dangerously deceptive to assume that Jesus could not have meant a Scriptural command simply because it is demanding. Many of Jesus' teachings are difficult and can only be accomplished through His power in you. But if you truly believe Jesus' words lead to life, you will find a way to obey rather than look for an excuse to disobey. When obedience is difficult, pray for His strength.

> The Spirit gives life; the flesh counts for nothing. The words I have spoken to you—they are full of the Spirit and life. —**John 6:63**

2. Can we say that we fully trust Jesus if we refuse to obey His teaching on a subject? Why or why not?

The cherry-picker approach: We cannot arbitrarily pick and choose passages we want to obey and ignore the rest. We must seek an understanding for *all* of Scripture. If all of Scripture is given to God's people for all time, we must have a consistent *system* to properly interpret and apply *every* passage.

We understand that some instructions in Scripture were cultural commands given to a specific group. Some were part of the Levitical Law that has already been fulfilled. Yet some are still binding for the Church today. How do we make that determination?

Every passage should be reckoned with. None should be overlooked. As we've learned, all of Scripture is given to God's people for all time, so we must have a *system* to properly interpret and apply *every* passage. All Christians and Christian faith traditions have parts of Scripture they don't encourage people to actively apply to their lives; but many do not have a consistent *system* in place for making those decisions.

If you're not applying or living out every directive in Scripture, you should have a solid reason why not. Your reason should be supported by the larger picture of Scripture.

3. Had you considered that you should have a consistent system in place for applying Scripture, rather than randomly enforcing commands based on preference? What are your thoughts about this?

A FIVE QUESTION SYSTEM FOR APPLYING SCRIPTURAL COMMANDS

Based upon the teachings of this course, following are five questions that can help you develop a system for applying all Scripture:

1. **Is the matter in question actually in the Bible, or is it a man-made tradition?** There is much theological debate about matters not addressed in Scripture. Disputed issues are often traditions, opinions or preferences—human ideas. They may be good ideas, but to elevate them to the status of Scripture is sinful. If it's an opinion or preference, state it as such. Don't treat it as a binding instruction of Scripture if it's not.

2. **What did Jesus and the Apostles teach on the matter?** Remember that Jesus and the Apostles have the final word on matters of faith and practice. (Reference *Days 23-24* for more information.)

3. **Is this an Old Testament Command that is no longer binding to a Christian?** What justification do you have for stating that this command is no longer binding? Did New Testament writers address it? Was it fulfilled though Christ? Was it carried on in New Testament practice? Was it prohibited in the New Testament? (Reference *Day 24* for more information.)

4 **What is the usefulness of this passage if it does not pertain to soul salvation?** Not all of Scripture is directly related to soul salvation, but it all has use. (Reference *Day 24* for examples.)

5. **Is this New Testament command a cultural instruction given to a specific group to address a specific cultural issue?** Some matters addressed in the early Church were reactions to cultural issues and were not specific commands for all times. Remember key questions to consider are: Were there different instructions given on the topic? What is the final word on the topic? (Reference *Day 23* for more information.)

acting on God's word

God will speak to you and provide direction; but the usefulness of what He reveals depends on your response. You must act on what He says and allow Him to change your thoughts, opinions and behavior.

GOOD GROUND: ACTING UPON GOD'S WORD

> Others, like seed sown on good soil, hear the word, accept it, and produce a crop—some thirty, some sixty, some a hundred times what was sown. —**Mark 4:20**

This happens when you consistently act on His Word; it produces a great harvest.

> Land that drinks in the rain often falling on it and that produces a crop useful to those for whom it is farmed receives the blessing of God. —**Hebrews 6:7**

For every part of Scripture that we reject, we reject life. But when we act upon Scripture, we can expect a harvest of the promises.

On *Day 26: How To Study Scripture*, we learned the importance of seeking *Illumination* and *Direction* from the Holy Spirit as we study Scripture. But knowing what you should do means nothing unless you actually do something about it. If you don't put God's direction into practice, you'll deceive yourself.

> Do not merely listen to the word, and so deceive yourselves. Do what it says. —**James 1:22**

The point of studying and reading Scripture isn't to increase your knowledge. It's to direct your behavior. Agreeing with Scripture is not the same as acting on Scripture.

For example: You can agree that God wants us to feed the hungry. You can read a verse and feel God is telling you to feed the hungry. You can even feel good about the idea of feeding the hungry. But until you actually give some food to someone who is hungry or donate some time or money to a group that feeds the hungry, you have not *acted* on the Word.

We deceive ourselves into thinking that agreeing with the Word is somehow acting upon the Word.

1. **In what ways can listening without action be deceptive?**

Jesus taught us that there will be many who hear His teachings but will not put them into practice. These people are building their life upon sand. When the storms of life come, they won't last. But those who hear *and obey* are building their lives upon a rock that will withstand the storms of life.

> "Therefore everyone who hears these words of Mine and acts on them, may be compared to a wise man who built his house on the rock. And the rain fell, and the floods came, and the winds blew and slammed against that house; and yet it did not fall, for it had been founded on the rock.
>
> Everyone who hears these words of Mine and does not act on them, will be like a foolish man who built his house on the sand. The rain fell, and the floods came, and the winds blew and slammed against that house; and it fell—and great was its fall." —**Matthew 7:24-27 NASB**

2. **What's the difference between hearing the Word and putting the Word into practice?**

We don't often reject God's Word outright. We begin applying it but give up when it gets hard, or we get busy and neglect it.

ROCKY GROUND: DIFFICULTY CAUSES US TO QUIT

> Others, like seed sown on rocky places, hear the word and at once receive it with joy. But since they have no root, they last only a short time. When trouble or persecution comes because of the word, they quickly fall away. —**Mark 4:16-17**

This happens when you receive the Word and begin to apply it but give up when life gets difficult. Applying God's Word can come at a great personal sacrifice to us, so when the "heat of the sun" burns down on us, we abandon the Word of God because we have not let it take "deep root" in our lives.

Quitting is not always a conscious decision; it can be a slow drift away from what you know you should do.

> We must pay the most careful attention, therefore, to what we have heard, so that we do not drift away. —**Hebrews 2:1**

3. Describe a way in which you started following a Scriptural command but slowly drifted away from it or quit because it became difficult.

THORNY GROUND: BUSYNESS CAUSES US TO QUIT

> Still others, like seed sown among thorns, hear the word; but the worries of this life, the deceitfulness of wealth and the desires for other things come in and choke the word, making it unfruitful. —**Mark 4:18-19**

This happens when you accept the Word, begin to apply it, but get distracted. Life is busy. There's no end to the things that demand your attention and vie for priority over applying God's Word. Jesus referred to this as allowing thorns to choke out the growth of His Word in your heart. We allow the cares and concerns of this life to stop us from acting upon God's Word.

> But land that produces thorns and thistles is worthless and is in danger of being cursed. In the end it will be burned. —**Hebrews 6:8**

4. Describe a way in which the busyness of life has distracted you from God's desires for you.

putting it together

So then, just as you received
Christ Jesus as Lord, continue
to live your lives in him.
— COLOSSIANS 2:6

DAY 29

living a Spirit-led life

In this workbook, we've learned ways in which to grow in our relationship with God through prayer, worship and Bible reading. Now we will learn how to incorporate these activities in our daily lives and grow.

It is vital that you realize that if God's Spirit is in you, then Christ is with you wherever you go. You must learn to maintain an ongoing conversation with Him throughout each day. This is what Paul referred to when he instructed his readers to pray continually (1 Thessalonians 5:17).

Jesus developed such an intimate relationship with God that He *only did* what He saw His Father *doing*. This means that God is actively at work in the world around us; we must become aware and join what God is doing.

> Jesus gave them this answer: "Very truly I tell you, the Son can do nothing by himself; he can do only what he sees his Father doing, because whatever the Father does the Son also does."
> —**John 5:19**

To truly cultivate a relationship with Christ, you must acknowledge His Presence and pursue His will in every situation. However, this type of awareness can only be developed by spending time alone with the Lord so that we can know His voice and hear it above the "noise" of the world around us.

> "My sheep listen to my voice; I know them, and they follow me." —**John 10:27**

130   GROWTH

Notice this instruction from Paul:

> Since we are living by the Spirit, let us follow
> the Spirit's leading in every part of our lives.
> —Galatians 5:25 NLT

1. **According to the verse, which part of your day is yours
   to keep? Which part of your day should be submitted
   to the Holy Spirit?**

Now read The *Message Translation's* description of Romans 12:1-2.
This paraphrase helps highlight and apply this passage in usable,
current language.

> So here's what I want you to do, God helping
> you: Take your everyday, ordinary life—your
> sleeping, eating, going-to-work, and walking-
> around life —and place it before God as an
> offering. Embracing what God does for you is
> the best thing you can do for him. Don't become
> so well-adjusted to your culture that you fit
> into it without even thinking. Instead, fix your
> attention on God. You'll be changed from the
> inside out. Readily recognize what he wants
> from you, and quickly respond to it. Unlike the
> culture around you, always dragging you down
> to its level of immaturity, God brings the best out
> of you, develops well-formed maturity in you.[46]

2. In what ways does this differ from what you believed God wanted from your life?

3   In what ways will understanding that all of your day belongs to God affect your attitude about your life, job, family, etc.?

Following are ways to give God your everyday life and pursue Him minute-by-minute:

- Place Holy Spirit reminders around your car, home, workspace, etc. to remind you that Christ is present. This can be done with sticky notes or by setting smart device reminders.

- When faced with a difficult or tempting situation, excuse yourself and take a few minutes to pray. If this occurs at work, go to the restroom or some other quiet place to be alone and pray.

- Be alert and pay attention to people around you. The Holy Spirit may ask you to encourage them or meet a need.

- The Holy Spirit may ask you to pray for others. If so, offer to pray for them. If they refuse, be polite and pray for them later on your own.

- Be mindful of negative influences. If people pull you into destructive conversations such as gossip or immoral topics, politely excuse yourself.

- See each task in front of you as an opportunity to serve God. Ask Him to work through you while working at your job, caring for your kids, volunteering, etc.

It may take some time for these approaches to become habit—but over time they will become a way of life.

4. List other ways the Holy Spirit may lead you during your day.

5. Place a few Holy Spirit reminders in places you'll see throughout the day. Practice the habit of acknowledging His Presence. Smart device reminders also work well for this. Where will you place your reminders?

intentional time with God

While you learn to involve the Holy Spirit in every part of your day, you should also set aside focused alone time with God. Intimacy grows through focused moments alone with the person you love.

For example, taking a few minutes to speak with your spouse alone over morning coffee or after the kids are in bed will increase your intimacy.

Likewise, it is vitally important to have space set aside in your day to spend time with God in prayer and Bible study.[47]

DAILY TIME WITH GOD

Consider spending a few minutes every day working through the *ID Method of Bible Study (Day 26)* and the *H.E.A.R.T. Pattern of Prayer (Day 8)*.

Escaping the noise: The problem is that most of our lives are too noisy and busy for us to truly listen. Learning to quiet yourself, clear your mind from distraction and listen to God may be very difficult. But forcing yourself into a calm or quiet environment for the sole purpose of interacting with God will produce phenomenal results. The Holy Spirit will speak in a powerful way if you take time and create space for Him.

> Come to me, all you who are weary and burdened, and I will give you rest.
> **—Matthew 11:28**

1. According to this verse, what will happen if you take time to come to God?

When Jesus came out of intense times of serving others, He withdrew to quiet places to pray. When He prepared for difficult tasks, most notably facing death on the cross, He withdrew and found strength by spending focused time alone with the Father.

> But Jesus often withdrew to lonely places and prayed. —Luke 5:16

There are numerous ways to do this. You might leave early for work and pull off the road somewhere in order to connect with God. You could get up in the morning before the family to commune with God. Some people designate a space in their home as a prayer closet. Others take daily prayer walks. The possibilities are as varied and unique as our personalities. Figure out what works for you and do it.

Your prayer and Bible study times do not need to happen together. Consider splitting them up if time is an issue. For example, try reading your Bible when you first get up in the morning and use your commute as time to pray.

2. Where and when will your listening space and time be?

3. Which obstacles will you need to overcome to create space and time for you and God alone?

Expectation: Daily time with God is something you can look forward to with excitement because you know that God will speak to you, lead you and guide you. You will get a concentrated dose of the Holy Spirit's influence in your life, which will transform the way you think, which will transform you. Do not be surprised when others begin to notice a difference.

Remember that your expectation determines your motivation. If you expect to get great spiritual benefit from time with God, you'll be more motivated to make and take the time.

4. Have you ever looked at time with God as something to approach with joy and anticipation? Why or why not?

5. In what ways do you expect that to be different now?

EXTENDED "SOAKING" TIMES WITH GOD

We've learned the importance of being aware of God's Presence *moment by moment*. We've learned the importance of setting time *daily* to interact with God. It's also important to plan *extended periods* of time for deep communion with God.

It's good to routinely (perhaps once a week) set aside a minimum of one or two hours for deep communion with God to "soak" in His Presence. See this time as a date with God. Do what you normally do in your daily prayer time but allow more time for "soaking" and listening.

This may be done where you spend your daily quiet time, or it could be somewhere else. Some churches host regular times or have prayer rooms set aside for extended prayer. If your church does not do this, consider helping alongside someone in your church to create and host a space for extended prayer.

6. When and where will you spend an extended time with God?

7. Does your church host a place/time for extended prayer? If no, how can you assist to create one? If yes, in what ways can you help maintain it?

YOUR TIME WITH GOD

Use this guide in both your daily time and extended times with God.

Recommended items to bring:

*   A Bible
*   A journal or notebook to write down ideas the Holy Spirit shares with you
*   Worship music that can help you stay focused and create an environment of worship

Begin with worship and prayer. Review the different expressions of worship you have learned on *Day 7*. Include as many of them as you can. Remember that you are initiating this time with God, so express your love for Him, regardless of how you feel at the moment.

Slowly work through the H.E.A.R.T. pattern of prayer.
(Reference *Day 8*)

*   **H**umble yourself before God
*   **E**mbrace His Will and Kingdom
*   **A**sk for today's needs
*   **R**eceive and give forgiveness
*   **T**urn from temptation

Sit quietly, listen, and respond to the Holy Spirit's promptings. "Soak" in His Presence. (Reference *Day 9*)

Read Scripture and "I.D." Jesus' voice in what you read.
(Reference *Day 26*)

*   **I**llumination: Ask Jesus to speak to you while you read. What is He highlighting to you?
*   **D**irection: What will you do based upon what you read? Ask the following questions:
    -   Is there an attitude or belief I need to change?
    -   Is there behavior I need to stop or one I need to start?
    -   Is there a promise to depend upon?
    -   Is there an idea or message I need to share with someone else?

Take time to carefully reflect on your life. Ask the Holy Spirit what needs to change.

If you fully engage during this time, it will soon become vital. You'll be motivated to spend increasing amounts of time in this "deep" place communing with God.

what's next?

Congratulations on making it to the end of this Workbook! You've gained valuable tools, skills and practices to help you grow in your relationship with God.

In the next book, *Workbook 4: Discover Relationships*, you will learn how to develop healthy, human relationships as well as work through past relational pain while you learn to approach relationships as a child of God.

You're on an exciting journey of discovering and growing in your identity as a child of God. Keep pushing forward!

> Brothers and sisters, I do not consider myself yet to have taken hold of it. But one thing I do: Forgetting what is behind and straining toward what is ahead, I press on toward the goal to win the prize for which God has called me heavenward in Christ Jesus.
> —**Philippians 3:13-14**

WORKBOOK 3:

growth checkpoint

Before you move on to *Workbook 4: Discover Relationships*, take a few minutes to evaluate how you're applying the principles learned in this Workbook:

1   **Have you set up a listening space to daily be with God? If yes, where? If not, what is keeping you from doing so?**

2. **Are you routinely studying Scripture and using the I.D. method? If yes, describe the ways it helps you better understand Scripture. If not, what is keeping you from regularly studying Scripture?**

3. **Are you learning to be aware of God's Presence with you at all times and involving His Presence in your everyday life? If yes, give a recent example.**

4. Are you taking **regular** times to have a "date" with God and soak in His Presence for extended periods of time? When was the last time you did this?

5. Are you regularly taking time to allow God to speak to you through His family, the Church? Give a recent example of how this happened. (Was it through Biblical teaching, a discussion, prayer, etc.?)

6. What attitudes or actions do you need to change based upon what you learned concerning God's intervention in the world?

7. Go back and review your *Plan for Change* from *Book 2: Discover Freedom*. When will you review this plan again with your accountability partner?

Be sure to go back and review any part of this Workbook about which you're unclear. Talk about it with your study group, Pastor or other spiritually mature Christians.

ENDNOTES

1 https://www.blueletterbible.org/lang/Lexicon/Lexicon.cfm?strongs=G3875&t=KJV

2 Don Cousins and Judson Poling. *Leader's Guide 1: Friendship with God, The Incomparable Jesus, and Follow Me.* Grand Rapids, MI: Zondervan, 1992.115-116.

3 This idea and others in this section were inspired by: Wimber, John. *Signs and Wonders and Church Growth.* Placentia, CA: Vineyard Ministries International, 1984. Section 4. Pg. 3-4

4 Acts 2:3; Acts 2:33; Acts 8:15-18: Acts 10:44; Acts 11:15; Acts 19:1-7

5 Acts 2:4; Acts 4:31; Acts 8:14-18; Acts 9:17; Acts 10:44-46; Acts 13:52; Acts 19:1-7

6 https://www.biblegateway.com/verse/en/Ephesians%205:18

7 This example was shared with the author by a friend, John Eklund.

8 C.S. Lewis, *Reflections on the Psalms.* New York: Harcourt, Brace & Co., 1958. Pg. 93–97

9 These ideas were made popular by: Chapman, Gary D. *The Five Love Languages: How to Express Heartfelt Commitment to Your Mate.* Chicago: Northfield Pub., 2004.

10 Lewis, Pg. 93-97

11 Song Lyrics. Greene, Keith. *Oh Lord, You're Beautiful.* Brentwood Benson Publishing. 1980

12 Richard Foster. *Celebration of Discipline: The Path to Spiritual Growth.* San Francisco: HarperOne, 2018. Pg. 7-8

13 Various online resources are available that can further explain, as well as give recipes and food options for those seeking to engage in a Daniel Fast.

14 1 Samuel 7:5-6, Ezra 8:21-23, Nehemiah 9:1-3, Joel 2:15-16, Jonah 3:5-10, Acts 27:33-37 are all examples of group fasts.

15 Edward Langton. *History of the Moravian Church; the Story of the First International Protestant Church.* London: Allen & Unwin, 1956.

16 Dan Graves. "Jeremy Lanphier Led Prayer Revival." Christianity.com. https://www.christianity.com/church/church-history/timeline/1801-1900/jeremy-lanphier-led-prayer-revival-11630507.html

[17] Mark Galli. "Revival at Cane Ridge." Christianity Today. https://www.christianitytoday.com/history/issues/issue-45/revival-at-cane-ridge.html

[18] Truth In History. "The Welsh Revival of 1904-1905." Truth in History. http://truthinhistory.org/the-welsh-revival-of-1904-1905-2.html

[19] Wikipedia. "Billy Graham." Wikipedia. https://en.wikipedia.org/wiki/Billy_Graham (accessed February 17, 2019). This article provides numerous other citations concerning the life and ministry of Billy Graham.

[20] Gregory A., and Edward K. Boyd. *Letters from a Skeptic: A Son Wrestles with His Fathers Questions about Christianity.* Colorado Springs: David C. Cook, 2008. Pg. 78-85

[21] Genesis 1:28

[22] Cousins and Poling, Pg. 96-97.

[23] This prayer is accredited to Reinhold Niebuhr. For a complete text of the prayer, go to https://www.celebraterecovery.com/resources/cr-tools/serenityprayer.

[24] Boyd and Boyd, Pg. 32-36

[25] Dr. Henry Cloud and John Townsend. "The Law of Reaping and Sowing." FaithGateway. https://www.faithgateway.com/the-law-of-reaping-and-sowing/#.XJ_x0y-ZOMA

[26] This idea came from a sermon preached at Saddleback Church by Brad Johnson entitled, *When Time Stands Still.* 2001

[27] Boyd and Boyd, Pg. 55-60

[28] http://wordcentral.com/cgi-bin/student?book=Student&va=bible

[29] The author does not take credit for the examples used in this section. Variations of these examples have circulated in Christian thought for some time. Go to the following website for more information and resources to support the validity and reliability of the Bible. https://www.truelife.org/answers/why-believe-the-bible-9b49ac25-c1c6-4e9c-92ee-095ea3fe1182.
Also reference Lee Strobel. *The Case for Christ.* Grand Rapids: Zondervan.com, 2016, and Lee Strobel. *The Case for Faith: A Journalist Investigates the Toughest Objections to Christianity.* Grand Rapids: Zondervan.com, 2000.

[30] Joel B. Green. *Seized by Truth: Reading the Bible as Christian Scripture.* Nashville: Abingdon Press. 2007. Pg. 51-53

[31] Gordon Fee and Douglas Stuart. *How to Read the Bible for all its Worth* (3rd ed.). Grand Rapids: Zondervan Publishing. 2003. Kindle Locations 692-732.

[32] Some English-speaking people are very loyal to the King James Version (KJV) of the Bible. However, to insist that it is the only translation inspired by God reveals a misunderstanding of the Bible and its translations. The King James Version is not the original version of the Bible. As noted, the original documents were written in Hebrew, Aramaic and Greek 2,000 to 4,000 years ago.

During the reign of King James of England there were several English translations of the Bible, but most were questionable or incomplete. King James wanted a complete, accurate translation for English-speaking people to use, so he commissioned various scholars to translate the ancient texts. The translation commissioned by and named for him was published in 1611.

The KJV was a good formal translation, but the English language has changed considerably over the four centuries since. It sounds very different. This makes the KJV difficult for modern audiences to read and easily understand. In addition to the language sounding different overall, many English words have different meanings and connotations today than they did in the 17th century. This could lead to the reader forming false conclusions by attaching a different meaning to a word than the original translators knew, intended and meant. It should be noted that several versions of the KJV translation have been developed in recent years to help remedy the language barriers. This would include the American King James Version.

As with all translations, it is recommended that you read and compare the KJV with a couple of other valid, formal or functional translations, to increase your overall grasp of the meaning and intention of the original text.

[33] Fee and Stuart, Kindle Locations 531-923

[34] https://www.blueletterbible.org/faq/don_stewart/don_stewart_273.cfm

[35] Francis Chan and Mark Beuving. *Multiply: Disciples Making Disciples.* Colorado Springs: David C. Cook. 2012. Pg. 124-126

[36] Ibid. Pg. 132-133

[37] Green, Pg. 51-53

[38] Fee and Stuart, Kindle Locations 506-519.

[39] Chan and Beuving, Pg. 135-136.

[40] Fee and Stuart, Kindle Location 1539.

[41] For an examination of how different Christian theologians, including Reformers Martin Luther and John Calvin have viewed the Law of Moses, go to: https://thenomocracyproject.wordpress.com/2015/03/23/luther-and-calvin-on-the-mosaic-law-by-john-d-wilsey/

[42] For suggestions with understanding and appropriating all of the Bible as Christian Scripture, consult the following books: Joel B. Green. *Seized by Truth: Reading the Bible as Christian Scripture.* Nashville: Abingdon Press, 2007. Gordon Fee and Douglas Stuart. *How to read the Bible for all its Worth* (3rd ed.). Grand Rapids: Zondervan Publishing, 2003. Kenneth Schenck. *A Brief guide to Biblical Interpretation* (2nd ed.). Marion: Triangle Publishing, 2008.

[43] Green, Pg. 78-79

[44] For different suggestions on different ways to study the Bible (e.g. topical, word study, character study, etc) read: Richard Warren. *Rick Warrens Bible Study Methods: Twelve Ways to Study the Bible on Your Own.* Grand Rapids: Zondervan, 2006.

[45] Cousins and Poling, Pg. 80

[46] THE MESSAGE, copyright © 1993, 2002, 2018 by Eugene H. Peterson. Used by permission of NavPress. All rights reserved. Represented by Tyndale House Publishers, Inc.

[47] Cousins and Poling, Pg. 108-111

Workbook 3: Growth Checkpoint —Icon made by Roundicons from Flaticon is licensed by Creative Commons BY 3.0

Discover Discipleship Course

1. IDENTITY

2. FREEDOM

3. GROWTH

4. RELATIONSHIPS

5. MISSION

6. ALIGNMENT

For purchasing information and bulk discounts
go to discoverdiscipleship.com

Made in the USA
Middletown, DE
14 September 2024

60474893R00086